PATTON
UNLEASHED

PATTON UNLEASHED

**PATTON'S THIRD ARMY AND THE BREAKOUT
FROM NORMANDY, AUGUST–SEPTEMBER 1944**

Tim Ripley

MBI

This edition first published in 2003 by MBI, an imprint of
MBI Publishing Company, Galtier Plaza, Suite 200, 380 Jackson Street, St. Paul,
MN 55101-3885, USA

MBI titles are also available at discounts in bulk quantity for industrial or sales-promotional use. For
details write to Special Sales Manager at Motorbooks International Wholesalers & Distributors,
Galtier Plaza, Suite 200, 380 Jackson Street, St. Paul, MN 55101-3885 USA.

ISBN: 0-7603-1447-0

Printed in China

Editorial and design:
The Brown Reference Group plc
8 Chapel Place
Rivington Street
London
EC2A 3DQ
UK

Senior Editor: Peter Darman
Editor: James Murphy
Proofreading: Matt Turner
Picture research: Andrew Webb, Susannah Jayes
Design: Anthony Cohen
Maps: Bob Garwood
Production: Alastair Gourlay

CONTENTS

Appendices

DEDICATION AND ACKNOWLEDGEMENTS

Dedication

This book is written in tribute to the ordinary soldiers of the US Third Army who made possible Lieutenant-General George Patton's victories in August and September 1944. In these two monumental months the Third Army lost 4849 men killed in action, had 24,585 wounded and 5092 were recorded as missing. Patton may have received the plaudits and glory for his victories, but the soldiers at the sharp end paid for them with blood and sweat.

Acknowledgement

I would like to thank the following for their help in getting this project off the ground. The hard-working library staff at the Royal United Services Institute in London; Roderick de Normann for his help directing me to primary source material; Neil Tweedie and Micky Brooks for helping me to understand World War II strategy; Peter Donnelly of The King's Own Regiment Museum for his help with my research; Major Hasse Resenbro of the Danish Guard's Hussar's Regiment for accompanying me to the scenes of Patton's victories; Simon Leng and Greggie Gang for supporting my interest in the defeat of Nazi Germany; and finally, Amanda Cahill for putting up with my obsessive approach to book writing and bringing me back down to earth.

Key to Maps

Military units – types

⊠ infantry

▰ armoured

▱ motorized infantry/panzergrenadier

🪂 parachute/airborne

◯ combat command

Military units – size

XXXXX ☐ army group

XXXX ☐ army

XXX ☐ corps

XX ☐ division

X ☐ brigade

III ☐ regiment

II ☐ battalion

⊠ Task Force A

Military unit colours

▮ German

▯ British and Commonwealth

▮ US

▮ French

Military movement

➤ atttack/advance (in national colours)

┅➤ retreat (in national colours)

Geographical symbols

──── road

• urban area

urban area

trees

·—·—·—·— national boundary

──── river

·—·—·—·— railway

⊓⊔⊓⊔ canal

List of Maps

INTRODUCTION

THE PATTON SPEECH

"We have the finest food, the finest equipment, the best fighting spirit; and the best men in the world. Why, by God, I actually pity those poor sons-of-bitches we're going up against."

At a US Army base in southern England in June 1944, thousands of Third Army soldiers are gathered around makeshift stage in a field. This scene had been repeated time and again over the previous month as the Third Army's flamboyant commander visited each of his major units in turn to prepare them for the coming invasion of Nazi-occupied Europe. As Lieutenant-General George S. Patton strides forward to climb up onto the stage, the band breaks into the "General's March" and military policemen snap to attention. The assembled soldiery rises to its feet.

"Be seated. Men, this stuff that some sources sling around about America wanting out of this war, not wanting to fight, is a crock of bullshit. Americans love to fight, traditionally. All real Americans love the sting and clash of battle. You are here today for three reasons. First, because you are here to defend your homes and your loved ones. Second, you are here for your own self-respect, because you would not want to be anywhere else. Third, you are here because you are real men and all real men like to fight. When you, everyone of you, were kids, you all admired the champion marble player, the

■ *Left:* General George S. Patton was famous for his barnstorming speeches. Though some of his contemporaries frowned upon his frequent use of coarse language, he believed it motivated his troops. In this he was right; his men loved it.

fastest runner, the toughest boxer, the big-league ball players and the All-American football players. Americans love a winner. Americans will not tolerate a loser. Americans despise cowards. Americans play to win all of the time. I wouldn't give a hoot in hell for a man who lost and laughed. That's why Americans have never lost nor will ever lose a war; for the very idea of losing is hateful to an American.

"You are not all going to die. Only two percent of you right here today would die in a major battle. Death must not be feared. Death, in time, comes to all men. Yes, every man is scared in his first battle. If he says he's not, he's a liar. Some men are cowards, but they fight the same as the brave men or they get the hell slammed out of them watching men fight who are just as scared as they

are. The real hero is the man who fights even though he is scared.

"Some men get over their fright in a minute under fire. For some, it takes an hour. For some, it takes days. But a real man will never let his fear of death overpower his honour, his sense of duty to his country, and his innate manhood. Battle is the most magnificent competition in which a human being can indulge. It brings out all that is best and it removes all that is base. Americans pride themselves on being He-Men and they ARE He-Men.

"Remember that the enemy is just as frightened as you are, and probably more so. They are not supermen.

"All through your army careers, you men have bitched about what you call 'chicken-shit drilling'. That, like everything else in this army, has a

■ **Above: Patton (left) built up an image of himself that was founded on a reputation for fearlessness and aggression. Like Napoleon, he made sure that he was seen on the battlefield, rallying his troops and providing them with the inspiration to fight on.**

■ *Above:* Patton's rousing speeches were not confined to his men. In his dealings with the press he was keen to enhance his image and reputation. He is seen here describing the Seine offensive to the press in typical style.

definite purpose. That purpose is alertness. Alertness must be bred into every soldier. I don't give a fuck for a man who's not always on his toes. You men are veterans or you wouldn't be here. You are ready for what's to come. A man must be alert at all times if he expects to stay alive. If you're not alert, at some time a German son-of-an-asshole-bitch is going to sneak up behind you and beat you to death with a sockful of shit!

"There are 400 neatly marked graves somewhere in Sicily, all because one man went to sleep on the job. But they are German graves, because we caught the bastard asleep before they did.

"An army is a team. It lives, sleeps, eats, and fights as a team. This individual heroic stuff is pure horseshit. The bilious bastards who write that kind of stuff for the *Saturday Evening Post* don't know any more about real fighting under fire than they know about fucking! We have the finest food, the finest equipment, the best spirit, and the best men in the world. Why, by God, I actually pity those poor sons-of-bitches we're going up against. By God, I do.

"My men don't surrender, and I don't want to hear of any soldier under my command being captured unless he has been hit. Even if you are hit, you can still fight back. That's not just bullshit, either. The kind of man that I want in my command is just like the lieutenant in Libya, who, with a Luger against his chest, jerked off his helmet, swept the gun aside with one hand, and busted the hell out of the Kraut with his helmet. Then he jumped on the gun and went out and killed another German before they knew what the hell was coming off. And, all of that time, this man had a bullet through a lung. There was a real man!

"All of the real heroes are not story-book combat fighters, either. Every single man in this army plays a vital role. Don't ever let up. Don't ever think that your job is unimportant. Every man has a job to do and he must do it. Every man is a vital link in the great chain. What if every truck driver suddenly decided that he didn't like the whine of those shells overhead, turned yellow, and jumped headlong into a ditch? The cowardly bastard could say: 'Hell, they won't miss me, just one man in thousands.' But, what if every man thought that way? Where in the hell would we be now? What would our country, our loved ones, our homes, even the world, be like? No, goddamnit, Americans don't think like that. Every man does his job. Every man serves the whole. Every department, every unit, is important in the vast scheme of this war.

"The ordnance men are needed to supply the guns and machinery of war to keep us rolling. The quartermaster is needed to bring up food and clothes

■ *Right:* **Patton (second from right), here a major-general, ashore at Fedhala, Morocco, on 9 November 1942, a day after the Allied landings. His successes during Operation Torch earned him much credit.**

because where we are going there isn't a hell of a lot to steal. Every last man on K.P. [key point] has a job to do, even the one who heats our water to keep us from getting the 'G.I. Shits'.

"Each man must not think only of himself, but also of his buddy fighting beside him. We don't want yellow cowards in this army. They should be killed off like rats. If not, they will go home after this war and breed more cowards. The brave men will breed more brave men. Kill off the goddamned cowards and we will have a nation of brave men. One of the bravest men that I ever saw was a fellow on top of a telegraph pole in the midst of a furious firefight in Tunisia. I stopped and asked what the hell he was doing up there at a

time like that. He answered, 'Fixing the wire, Sir.' I asked, 'Isn't that a little unhealthy right about now?' He answered, 'Yes Sir, but the goddamned wire has to be fixed.' I asked, 'Don't those planes strafing the road bother you?' And he answered, 'No, Sir, but you sure as hell do!' Now, there was a real man. A real soldier. There was a man who devoted all he had to his duty, no matter how seemingly insignificant his duty might appear at the time, no matter how great the odds.

"And you should have seen those trucks on the road to Tunisia. Those drivers were magnificent. All day and all night they rolled over those son-of-a-bitching roads, never stopping, never faltering from their course, with shells

■ *Above left:* **Patton (left) goes over battle plans with one of his Third Army corps commanders, General Manton S. Eddy.**

■ *Above:* **In a typical Patton style, Major-General Robert W. Grow, commander of the 6th Armored Division, addresses his men** *en masse.*

bursting all around them all of the time. We got through on good old American guts. Many of those men drove for over 40 consecutive hours. These men weren't combat men, but they were soldiers with a job to do. They did it, and in one hell of a way they did it. They were part of a team. Without team effort, without them, the fight would have been lost. All of the links in the chain pulled together and the chain became unbreakable.

"Don't forget, you men don't know that I'm here. No mention of that fact is to be made in any letters. The world is not supposed to know what the hell happened to me. I'm not supposed to be commanding this army. I'm not even supposed to be here in England. Let the first bastards to find out be the goddamned Germans. Some day I want to see them raise up on their piss-soaked hind legs and howl, 'Jesus Christ, it's the goddamned Third Army again and that son-of-a-fucking-bitch Patton.' We want to get the hell over there. The quicker we clean up this goddamned mess, the quicker we can take a little jaunt against the purple-pissing Japs and clean out their nest, too. Before the goddamned Marines get all of the credit.

"Sure, we want to go home. We want this war over with. The quickest way to get it over with is to go get the bastards who started it. The quicker they are whipped, the quicker we can go home. The shortest way home is through Berlin and Tokyo. And when we get to Berlin I am personally going to shoot that paper-hanging son-of-a-bitch Hitler. Just like I'd shoot a snake!

"When a man is lying in a shell hole, if he just stays there all day, a German will get to him eventually. The hell with that idea. The hell with taking it. My men don't dig foxholes. I don't want them to. Foxholes only slow up an offensive. Keep moving. And don't give the enemy time to dig one, either. We'll win this war, but we'll win it only by fighting and by showing the Germans that we've got more guts than they have; or ever will have.

"War is a bloody, killing business"

"We're not going to just shoot the sons-of-bitches, we're going to rip out their living goddamned guts and use them to grease the treads of our tanks. We're going to murder those lousy Hun cocksuckers by the bushel-fucking-basket. War is a bloody, killing business. You've got to spill their blood, or they will spill yours. Rip them up the belly. Shoot them in the guts. When shells are hitting all around you and you wipe the dirt off your face and realize that instead of dirt it's the blood and guts of what once was your best friend beside you, you'll know what to do!

"I don't want to get any messages saying, 'I am holding my position.' We are not holding a goddamned thing. Let the Germans do that. We are advancing constantly and we are not interested in holding onto anything, except the enemy's balls. We are going to twist his balls and kick the living shit out of him all of the time. Our basic plan of operation is to advance and to keep on advancing regardless of whether we have to go over, under, or through the enemy. We are going to go through him like crap through a goose; like shit through a tin horn!

"Pushing means fewer casualties"

"From time to time there will be some complaints that we are pushing our people too hard. I don't give a good goddamn about such complaints. I believe in the old and sound rule that an ounce of sweat will save a gallon of blood. The harder we push, the more Germans we will kill. The more Germans we kill, the fewer of our men will be killed. Pushing means fewer casualties. I want you all to remember that. There is one great thing that you men will all be able to say after this war is over and you are home once again. You may be thankful that 20 years from now when you are sitting by the fireplace with your grandson on your knee and he asks you what you did in the great World War II, you won't have to cough, shift him to the other knee and say, 'Well, your Granddaddy shovelled shit in Louisiana.' No, Sir, you can look him straight in the eye and say, 'Son, your Granddaddy rode with the Great Third Army and a son-of-a-goddamned-bitch named Georgie Patton!'"

■ *Right:* General Patton strikes a determined pose. The image he portrayed to the public was no smokescreen. Patton had supreme self-confidence in his own abilities.

CHAPTER 1

PATTON – THE MAN

"And when you see General Patton ... you get the same feeling as when you saw Babe Ruth standing up to the plate. Here's a big guy who's going to kick the hell out of something."

US Navy lieutenant watching Patton land in France, July 1944.

George Smith Patton is perhaps the most famous US combat general of the twentieth century. His exploits as an aggressive and hard-charging armoured commander during World War II are firmly established in military legend. Patton's place in history is more than assured by his battlefield exploits, but his larger-than-life persona meant that he was one of the first military media celebrities of the modern era.

Post-war audiences were exposed to the Patton phenomenon thanks in large part to the 1970 movie, *Patton*, which starred George C. Scott in his Oscar-winning lead role. Much of the dialogue in the movie faithfully drew on Patton's famous morale-inspiring speeches, making it one of Hollywood's more authentic products.

Patton carefully cultivated his image with the American public and among his troops to boost morale and establish

■ *Left:* General Patton (second from left) and the legendary British commander General Montgomery (far right) share a convivial moment. With them are General Dempsey (far left) and General Bradley (second from right).

moral dominance over his enemies. Some of his rivals in the US and British armies dismissed him as a "showman" because of his flashy uniforms, polished helmet and ivory-handled pistols, but beneath the brash exterior was a thoughtful, intelligent and very professional soldier.

The US Third Army's campaign in France during August and September 1944 was the pinnacle of Patton's military career. His rampage across France sealed the fate of the German Army in Normandy, and has become a textbook example of how to employ armoured forces. In this book we look at that campaign in detail, explaining the role of Patton and his army in the successful Allied break-out from the Normandy bridgehead.

Everything in Patton's background seemed to predestine him for high military command. He was born in 1885 into a well-to-do California family, which could trace its roots back to service with the Confederate state of Virginia. Patton's grandfather had risen to be a colonel in the Confederate Army

and died in battle against Union troops in 1864. Fifteen other members of the Patton family fought for the Confederacy, and two others also died for the doomed Southern cause.

Other ancestors had helped found the young republic almost a century before, and fought against the British in the Revolutionary War (1775–83). Patton's orphaned father had followed family tradition and attended the famous Virginia Military Institute (VMI), before heading to California to make his fortune.

Patton – the soldier

The young George S. Patton soon set his heart on following in his grand-father's footsteps and devoting his life to a quest for military glory. After spending a year at VMI, he secured a coveted place at the West Point Military Academy outside New York. Over-coming dyslexia, after winning his commission he proved a successful cadet and opted to join the US Cavalry.

Coming from the West Coast, and having a wealthy background, made Patton unusual amongst the somewhat dour and egalitarian US Army of the early twentieth century. From his earliest days as a West Point cadet he was convinced he was destined to lead armies into battle, and groomed himself for this task. The young Patton read military history prodigiously, and toured Civil War battlefields to try to understand how the "Great Captains" of that conflict had planned and fought their battles. Although he was sometimes accused of having an aristocratic manner, Patton was no military reactionary who idolized "horse cavalry". Coming from California he was firmly at home with the latest technology and gadgets of that era, owning a motor car before a horse. He was widely travelled in Europe,

■ *Right:* A young lieutenant named Patton (fifth from left) stands with other officers, including General John J. Pershing (fourth from left), in Mexico circa 1916–17.

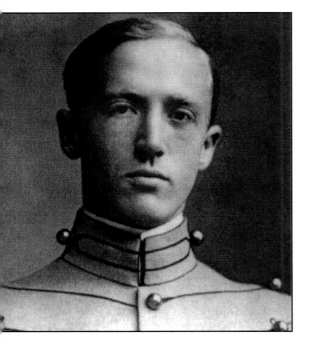

■ *Left:* George S. Patton Jr. as a West Point cadet. He graduated 46th out of a class of 103, and enrolled into the cavalry.

■ *Right:* Patton saw some of the fighting during World War I. He was injured in March 1918 while walking alongside his tanks, directing their fire.

representing the USA in the Olympic Pentathlon in 1912, training at the French Cavalry School and speaking French with an almost faultless accent.

Patton's first brush with death and military fame came during the US Army's 1916 punitive campaign in Mexico, when he led a motor car patrol that killed two prominent supporters of the bandit chief Pancho Villa. Patton boasted that he "initiated motorized warfare in the US Army".

After America's entry into World War I, Patton immediately volunteered to serve in France with General John "Black Jack" Pershing's expeditionary force. The British Army's use of tanks in 1917 at the Battle of Cambrai convinced Pershing that they were the decisive land weapon of the war, and he soon persuaded the US Army hierarchy to raise a tank corps. Until plans to build new tanks in the US came to fruition, the Americans had to rely on French-made two-man Renault light tanks.

The job of translating Pershing's ambitions into reality was given to the 32-year-old Major Patton in the winter of 1917. In a matter of weeks he had set up the US Army's first tank training school, written tactical manuals and begun organizing the first tank units. By the late spring, Patton had command of the first US Army tank brigade that was preparing to participate in the coming offensive against the Germans.

Pershing's American Expeditionary Force (AEF) went into action during September 1918, retaking the territory that the German forces had seized during the crushing Saint-Mihiel Offensive of March 1918, with Patton's 304th Tank Brigade in the lead. The primitive nature of the Renault tanks meant they had to be commanded by Patton walking alongside and indicating targets. Undaunted by this task, Patton led his tanks into battle with great zeal, but became so carried away with the battle that he lost communications with the commander of the Tank Corps, Brigadier-General S.D. Rockenbach. The general was not happy, but Patton was allowed to remain in command and again led his brigade into action during the US Army's Meuse-Argonne Offensive in September 1918 that brought the war to a victorious end for the Allies. Patton was less lucky this time, and was wounded by German shellfire leading his tanks forward.

By the time Patton had recuperated sufficiently to "break out" of a military hospital to get back into action, the war was over. Thanks to his recent combat experience, it was intended that Patton would play a key role in the formation of the peacetime US Army Tank Corps, helping to design the new tanks for America's army. The rush to disarm meant that Congress disbanded the Tank Corps in 1919 and scrapped the new tanks before they were built. The remaining tanks were transferred to the

■ *Below left:* **Patton almost single-handedly created the US Tank Corps. The unit was equipped with primitive Renault tanks, seen here.**

infantry and Congress reduced the size of the US Army to such an extent that thousands of regular army officers, such as Patton, had to accept demotions to stay in the service (at its height the AEF had just over two million men in 1918; in June 1921 Congress ordered the army to be reduced to a total of 150,000 men). Patton briefly served in one of the remaining tank units before it was disbanded, and so he decided to return to horse soldiering.

The 1920s and early 1930s were a depressing time for America's professional soldiers like Patton, who had to endure tedious garrison duty in remote corners of the country, or find themselves hunting elusive guerrillas in the jungles of the Philippines. Patton spent the interwar period moving from one

remote military post to another. Although he maintained an interest in tank developments, cooperating with the maverick tank designer Walter Christie and writing articles for military journals on armoured warfare, he was a long way from being at the centre of debates on the future of the US Army. At times Patton became convinced that his army career was going to finish ingloriously in peaceful retirement.

Patton's fortunes began to look up in the late 1930s, as war clouds started to gather over Europe. German Blitzkrieg campaigns in Poland and France were won by massed tank formations, forcing the US Army and Congress to wake up to the potential of the tank. As a result, the Armored Force was formed in July 1940. New tank designs were ordered, and officers with first-hand experience in armoured warfare suddenly found themselves in demand.

Honing the Tank Corps

Colonel Patton was called upon by the new chief of staff of the US Army, George C. Marshall, to take over command of the newly formed 2nd Armored Brigade, and then the 2nd "Hell on Wheels" Armored Division.

For over a year Patton drilled his new armoured troopers in the rigours of tank warfare. Once they had gained experience using their unreliable tanks, Patton took his men on gruelling exercises to practise the daring outflanking moves that would be a hallmark of his later campaigns. The pinnacle of Patton's efforts were the September 1941 Louisiana Maneuvers, which saw his division show that it was the best tank unit in the US Army. After the Japanese attacked Pearl Harbor on 7 December 1941, the US Army underwent a massive expansion and it was little surprise that the dynamic Patton was given command of I Armored Corps. He took the formation

out to the Arizona desert to prepare it for deployment to Africa to fight Field Marshal Erwin Rommel's Afrika Korps.

Major-General Patton was soon selected to play a leading role in Operation Torch, the Anglo-American landings in French North Africa. He was in charge of the force that was to seize Casablanca in November 1942. After only sporadic resistance, Patton was able to negotiate the surrender of the French garrison, and he then set about waiting for the order to advance to engage the Germans and Italians. After kicking his heels in Casablanca for three months, Patton was soon thrust into the battle for Tunisia, but not under ideal circumstances.

An advance US element, II Corps, had pushed close up to the Tunisian

■ *Above:* General Montgomery in his Surrey home before the invasion of Sicily. Patton and "Monty" crossed paths many times during the war, but despite their bitter rivalry, they were a fearsome team.

border at the Kasserine Pass, but was then ferociously driven back by Rommel's panzers that were advancing against the town of Thala. The US forces suffered terribly, with the loss of nearly 2000 men and huge numbers of tanks and other vehicles. Patton was given the job of sorting out the mess and restoring the reputation of the US forces in Africa. Within hours of his arrival at the demoralized force, he had started making his trademark morale-boosting speeches, sacked incompetent staff officers and begun preparing plans to attack the Germans.

By the end of March, Patton's troops were ready for action and, after they repulsed another panzer attack, morale soared. Now Patton went on the attack, with some success. As far as the American public were concerned Patton was a hero. Patton, however, thought his troops could have played a more prominent role in the defeat of the Afrika Korps, and privately fumed that the famous commander of the British Eighth Army, Bernard Montgomery, received the bulk of the glory. Within

the US Army, Patton's reputation as a "can-do" general was established and he was earmarked to command the US Seventh Army during the invasion of Sicily. He was now equal in status to Bernard Montgomery.

Operation Husky, the codename for the invasion of Sicily in July 1943, saw Patton and Montgomery land troops on the southern coast of the island. The Germans immediately counterattacked, pinning the invasion force into a narrow bridgehead. The British Ultra code-breaking operation soon informed Patton that he was only facing predominately weak Italian forces, so he decided to strike westwards to Palermo and then turn back eastwards to advance along the island's north coast to seize the key port of Messina and trap the bulk of the German forces facing the British.

When German troops tried to counterattack, Patton's men held their ground and amphibious landings were made to bypass German roadblocks on the precarious northern coast road. In less than a week Patton was at Messina waiting for the British. The Germans

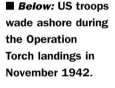

■ *Below:* US troops wade ashore during the Operation Torch landings in November 1942.

lost 100,000 men, the Italians up to 100,000, mostly prisoners. This was the first "all-American" victory in Europe and Patton's reputation was now at its zenith. Within a matter of days, however, he was facing dismissal and disgrace after slapping a GI he found in a field hospital suffering from "battle fatigue". The story leaked to the press and there were calls for Patton's dismissal.

The American supreme commander in Europe, General Dwight D. Eisenhower, however, was not going to lose one his top commanders in such a way. "Patton is indispensable to the war effort – one of the guarantors of our victory," he declared. Patton was ordered by Ike to apologize to the soldier concerned and to

■ *Above left:* General George C. Marshall, US Army chief of staff.

■ *Left:* General Dwight D. Eisenhower (left), affectionately known as "Ike", and General Erskine.

■ *Above:* **Advanced students of the Armored Force advance from their tanks under the cover of a smokescreen during training manoeuvres at Fort Knox, Kentucky.**

every major unit in the Seventh Army. For the rest of 1943 Patton was kept in limbo in the Mediterranean theatre as a decoy, making high-profile tours of local capitals to keep the Germans thinking the Allies would strike in Greece, southern France or anywhere else that took their fancy. This was Patton's punishment. For the remainder of the war he would always feel he was on "probation" for the slapping incident, and on several occasions Patton would

acquiesce in orders with which he disagreed, especially in the planning of how to attack into the Rhineland, simply to avoid risking dismissal.

In January 1944, he flew secretly to Scotland to take command of the US Third Army, which was preparing for Operation Overlord, the invasion of France. Patton had been reprieved. The US chief of staff, General George C. Marshall, compared the characters of Patton and Omar Bradley, who as First

■ *Left:* Brigadier-General Otto Weyland, commander of the US Army Air Force's XIX Tactical Air Command. "Opie" and Patton enjoyed an excellent relationship, which undoubtedly contributed to the Third Army's success.

Army commander would go ashore in Europe first. "Bradley will lead the invasion, but he is a limited objective general," said Marshall. "When we get moving, Patton is the man with the drive and imagination to do dangerous things fast."

Over the next 18 months as commander of the Third Army, Patton indeed set a bruising pace for both himself and his men. His style of command was unlike anything experienced by the US Army before or since. The showmanship of his barnstorming speeches and ivory-handled pistols had caught the public's imagination, but Patton was a serious professional soldier, with highly innovative tactics, and understood how to use both armour and airpower to decisive effect.

Patton took a great interest in military history and tried to draw lessons from the campaigns of the "Great Captains". He was also widely travelled around Europe, having conducted a motor-car tour of Brittany and Normandy, and so was personally familiar with much of the ground his troops would fight over.

From his experience in World War I and US armoured exercises in the early 1940s, Patton was convinced of the need to use tanks aggressively and *en masse* to secure strategic objectives, rather than to support infantry attacks. He was also a firm believer in manoeuvre warfare, constantly keeping his opponent on his toes and off-balance. Rather than engaging in attritional frontal attacks against the main enemy defences, Patton

■ *Above:* US generals (left to right) Jacob L. Devers, Jonathan W. Anderson and George S. Patton on an inspection tour of the troops in North Africa.

saw that victory could come from advancing deep behind enemy lines at great speed. As long as Patton's troops kept moving, the enemy would not be able to regain his balance and rebuild his defences. At the same time, Patton believed that the main target of the Allied invasion force should be the destruction of the German Army in France, rather than just the occupation of cities or ports.

To put his theories into practice, Patton had to abandon the hidebound command methods of the old US Army, based on written orders and close supervision of subordinates. He believed in "mission command" rather than issuing detailed orders; "Never tell people how to do things, tell them what to do and they will surprise you with their ingenuity."

The Third Army's staff officers were trained to issue brief, one-page orders prior to set-piece combat operations. Most of the key information was contained on map traces, giving objectives, routes and boundaries. With this information, subordinate commanders were supposed to use their initiative to plan and conduct their own operations. Patton would then issue verbal orders over the radio or during flying visits to the front to update subordinates to any changes in his battle plans.

In the run-up to major attacks, Patton would gather his staff together and brainstorm a solution. Much like a university professor, he would preside over these meetings wearing his glasses and taking brief notes until a consensus

■ *Left:* Patton's chief of staff, Hugh J. Gaffey, was the second most powerful man in the Third Army. Patton relied on Gaffey to keep the Third Army well oiled, and he was one of the few men in whom Patton had unshakeable faith.

was reached. Then the plan would become Patton's and he would drive his troops forward. Patton took great pains to include all his senior staff in his planning meetings and took notice of their views.

The role of intelligence

Usually Patton's intelligence staff officer, or G-2 chief, Colonel Oscar Koch, would take the floor first with the latest information on the enemy. Although security precautions prevented Ultra transcripts of German radio traffic being discussed at these meetings, Patton knew Koch used information passed to him from a British Ultra liaison team based in the Third Army's headquarters to prepare his intelligence assessments. From his experiences in Sicily, Patton knew the value of Ultra and was one of the few Allied commanders who used it to plan his operations at a tactical level.

Unlike some of his counterparts, Patton took intelligence very seriously, leading one of his intelligence officers to comment: "Patton never made a move without first consulting G-2. In planning, G-2 always had the first say. The usual procedure at other head-quarters was to decide what to do and then, perhaps, ask G-2 what was out in front. Patton always got his information first and acted on the basis of it. That explains why the Third Army was never surprised and why it always smashed through vulnerable sectors in the enemy's lines."

Ultra, however, was not foolproof, and in the French campaign the disorganized nature of the German retreat meant isolated units often could not communicate with their head-quarters by radio, making it impossible for Allied eavesdroppers to find out what they were doing or where they were.

The next most important man in Patton's command team was the commander of the US Army Air Force's XIX Tactical Air Command, Brigadier-General Otto Weyland. "Opie" commanded the P-47 Thunderbolt and P-51 Mustang ground-attack squadrons assigned to support the Third Army, and his headquarters was co-located next to Patton's own headquarters. Staff officers in the intelligence and operations branches shared joint command tents to ensure airpower and ground forces were fully synchronized. "We planned and executed our respective responsibilities in the closest coordination," said Wey-land. "From an early attitude of scepticism, General Patton went to the other extreme. He thought the XIX Tactical Command could do no wrong."

The importance of air support

Patton recognized that every ground manoeuvre by the Third Army had to be covered by air support, and went to great lengths to ensure Weyland's planes were always where they were needed. The airman was soon a close member of Patton's inner circle, drinking bourbon whiskey late into the night with the general and supporting him against senior Allied air commanders, who wanted airpower to operate indepen-dently of the ground forces. "We had a basic understanding," said Weyland, "that he [Patton] would run the ground and I would run the air."

It was clear to Patton that his Third Army was not operating in a vacuum, and he took a great interest in what was happening in neighbouring Allied armies, commanded by Montgomery, Omar Bradley and later Courtney Hodges. Liaison officers were posted to their headquarters with orders to hoover up as much information as possible to give Patton advance notice of important developments. This allowed him to set his staff to work so he could be ready with contingency plans long before rival Allied commanders even knew what to do.

Although Patton took seriously his "mission command" philosophies and rarely interfered with his subordinates' day-to-day activities, he liked to have a fingertip feel for what was happening on the battlefield. Recognizing that the traditional passing of written reports up the chain of command would not do in a fast-moving tank battle, Patton set up a special unit, the 6th Cavalry Group, known as Patton's Household Cavalry, to report personally to him, bypassing several layers of command. Much like Montgomery's "Phantom" organization, the 6th Cavalry under Colonel Edward M. Fickett dispatched small, radio-equipped scout teams throughout the Third Army's area of responsibility. They reported direct to a radio team that always travelled with Patton. Using their long-range radios, they could reach Patton at any hour of the day or night with the latest information on how the battle was going.

Knowing that he could always keep in touch with "battle-winning information" thanks to the 6th Cavalry, Patton never considered himself tied to his command van in his headquarters. He would spend his day touring his army's units in his jeep or Piper Cub light observation aircraft, leaving his faithful chief of staff, Major-General Hugh J. Gaffey, in charge of the Third

■ *Above:* General Patton holds a stage-managed "chat" with American invasion troops at an army camp in Great Britain prior to D-Day. Though the Third Army was not involved in the invasion, Patton made sure his men were ready for war.

Army's tactical headquarters, "Lucky Forward". Gaffey and his deputy, Brigadier-General Hobart R. Gay, were the most powerful men in the Third Army after Patton, and they kept his headquarters running like a well-oiled machine, as well as smoothing the wheels with higher echelons of command. Patton trusted them implicitly to make decisions in his absence, or take over command of the Third Army if he was killed.

As a result of these efforts Patton had unparalleled situational awareness of what was happening around him, which was essential when conducting a fast-moving campaign. This meant that, even when out on the road visiting his troops, he felt confident enough to make snap decisions to redirect his army to new objectives, even when based on the scantiest information. To some less perceptive colleagues in the US and Allied armies, it seemed as if Patton was not a serious soldier because he behaved like a gadfly, darting around the battlefield. Patton, however, was always one step ahead of his enemies and rivals.

At the heart of Patton's method of command was his unique way of motivating his troops to fight. The wartime media made great play of his dramatic persona and theatrical speeches, but Patton carefully cultivated his image. Unlike many US generals of the era who tried to portray themselves as "just an ordinary joe", Patton deliberately chose to be aloof from his men. As a Southern aristocrat, Patton was not interested in trying to be a "democratic general" or "a man of the people". He wanted to project the image of being an aggressive, hard-charging general, who wanted to win but who was not going to squander his men's lives needlessly.

"No bastard every won a war by dying for his country, they won it by making the other poor dumb bastard die for his," summed up Patton's philosophy. His troops loved it. His famous speech prior to D-Day (see

■ *Below:* British and American troops intermingle in the Somme area in mid-1944. When the Third Army was committed to France, Patton's morale-boosting efforts paid dividends.

■ *Left:* **Critics have claimed that Patton was a mere showman, interested only in vainglorious pursuits of victory and his own image. However, this harsh criticism does not take into account his genuine military genius and concern for the troops under his command.**

Introduction) was carefully crafted by Patton to push all the right buttons and create the impression that the members of the Third Army were an élite formation, led by a warrior who knew what he was doing. His reputation as the "conqueror of Sicily" added to his image as a winner, and Patton was keen to make his troops know they were now part of a winning team. (In 38 days US and British troops had killed or wounded approximately 29,000 enemy soldiers and captured over 140,000 more; American losses totalled 2237 killed and 6544 wounded and captured. The British suffered 12,843 casualties, including 2721 dead.) "A man with guts but no brain is only half a soldier," he would tell his men. "We licked the Germans in Africa and Sicily because we had brains as well as guts."

Man management

Patton insisted on the Third Army having its own distinctive insignia, and all troops under his command had to abide by his strict dress code. The rest of the Allied forces in France could dress like slobs, but Patton's Third Army was going to look like soldiers at all times!

Patton's appearances among his troops during the build-up to the D-Day landings were carefully stage-managed to show the general in a good light. It was not Patton's style to mingle with his troops in cookhouses or cinema halls, making small talk.

He would stride onto large stages and effectively let everyone known he was the boss. Some senior US Army generals were shocked by Patton's unorthodox approach and frequent blaspheming, but he was unrepentant. The aim was to motivate his troops in language they understood. Some took a lot more convincing than others, with one commenting after a Patton speech in which he talked about wars being won by blood and guts. "Yeah, his blood, our guts … big deal." The name stuck and Patton became known as "Old Blood and Guts". One GI commented after hearing a Patton speech, "Here was a man for whom you would go to hell and back."

A frontline general

Once the Third Army moved into France, Patton's leadership style evolved to meet the new situation. He would spend as much time as possible out visiting units, rather than remaining in the comfort of his headquarters.

He would appear at all hours of the day to make impromptu speeches or issue orders in person to unit commanders. Patton was always dressed immaculately in riding breaches, with his ivory-handled pistols displayed prominently and his white bull terrier dog, Willie, at his side. While stories of Patton standing up in the middle of fields during German air raids are the stuff of legend, he certainly tried to give off an air of confidence wherever he went to reinforce the image that he was in command and knew what he was doing.

Patton's aides always travelled with a box full of medals and rank badges, so that the general could instantly decorate or promote troops in the field.

He has been accused of revelling in war, especially after comments such as "Compared to war all human activities are futile, if you like war as I do." Patton, however, never showed this side of him to his troops. He took great interest in looking after his wounded soldiers, and on several occasions administered first aid and morphine to casualties.

The results of these efforts were amazing. Third Army troops idolized their commander and made great play of being "Georgie's boys". As the Third Army rampaged across France, morale soared. Their general had lived up to his hype, giving his troops victory with minimal American casualties.

CHAPTER 2

PATTON'S ARMY

"Everyone has to 'lead in person'. A commander who failed to obtain his objectives and who was not dead or severely wounded has not done his full duty."

Patton, briefing to Third Army officers, England, March 1944

The story of Patton's Third Army is illustrative of the dramatic expansion of the US Army in three short years from peacetime garrison force into an offensive army *par excellence*.

After being activated in World War I and participating in the occupation of Germany until 1919, the US Third Army was disbanded. During the 1930s it was reformed to administer US Army units in the southeast of the USA. During the early years of World War II it was transformed into a training organization, responsible for preparing divisions for combat overseas at the huge Louisiana manoeuvre area. In December 1943, it was officially designated as the headquarters of a combat army, and ordered to prepare to deploy overseas for the invasion of Europe. Little more than a month later, the advance party of the headquarters was on its way to Scotland aboard the cruise liner RMS *Queen Mary*, and the bulk of the staff followed shortly after on the *Ile de France*.

■ *Left:* One of the more unusual weapons of World War II – a 4.5in multiple rocket-launcher mounted on an M4A3 Sherman tank, this one from the 14th Armored Division. Rocket launchers were excellent for saturating an area with high explosive.

Waiting in England for his new staff was Patton. The old commander, Lieutenant-General Courtney Hodges, had been transferred in preparation for taking over the US First Army, leaving Patton to put his mark on his new command. In the course of the next four months more than 250,000 soldiers followed across the Atlantic Ocean to fill out the Third Army's order of battle. By June 1944, Patton had four US and one French armoured division, and eight American infantry divisions under his command.

Patton's GIs

These formations were manned almost exclusively by conscripted Americans who had been drafted in the months following the attack on Pearl Harbor. In a matter of weeks, the strength of the US Army had reached some 1.4 million men. The senior officer ranks were made up of regular soldiers, like Patton, with years of experience stretching back to World War I, but they were few and far between. Middle-ranking battalion and company grade officers were mostly graduates of the Reserve Officers Training Corps or National Guard veterans. Few had combat experience.

The draft had been introduced in 1940 with the passing of the Selective Service Act, but only a small fraction of the potential 900,000 draftees had been called to serve "Uncle Sam". During the first months after Pearl Harbor, the US Army was preoccupied with setting up the basic training infrastructure necessary to expand to its target strength of 72 divisions.

First port of call for draftees was a 17-week-long boot camp where they were taught the basics of soldiering, from shooting to saluting and field hygiene. Known as Replacement Training Centers, these also prepared draftees for service with their intended branch of the army – armour, infantry,

artillery and so on. The final phase of a GI's training would take place with a specialist service to prepare him for assignment to his unit. Here tank crewmen, infantrymen, artillery gunners and radio signalmen learned their skills prior to posting. For units forming in the US during the early years of World War II, a cycle of battalion, regimental, divisional and corps exercises was undertaken to prepare them for action overseas. Unlike in the Korean and Vietnam wars in the 1950s, 1960s and 1970s, the units formed at this time generally stayed together until the end of the war, under the command of the same officers. This was the basis for sound unit cohesion and allowed training to be conducted to a very high level. Once committed to action, however, units were "drip-fed" replacements from a large pool assigned to the European theatre. This meant that as the campaign in northwest Europe

■ *Above:* **A young American recruit takes his oath of allegiance before beginning his 17-week boot camp.**

progressed, the character and spirit of many US units changed dramatically as casualties took their toll.

The rapid expansion of the US Army obviously led to major growing pains, associated with a huge influx of new recruits to an organization lacking in equipment, bases and experienced officers. It took time for units to start to spark and begin to gel together. A rotation through the Louisiana manoeuvre area was usually the culmination of training for the units of the Third Army. Here draconian umpires, led by Lieutenant-General Walter Kreuger, put both officers and men through a gruelling series of military exercises.

Once Patton's troops arrived in Great Britain, he engaged them in a further round of training to improve their personal skills and ability to operate together in large operations. As the Third Army was not allocated to be in the first wave of the invasion, its troops did not have to train to assault the Normandy beaches. Patton therefore concentrated on drilling his men to make deep penetrating manoeuvres behind enemy lines, driving along the narrow British roads and rapidly building tactical bridges to cross rivers, to maintain the overall momentum of the advance.

Tank units and infantry then had to learn how to fight in the closed confines of the European countryside, rather than on the open expanses of the American prairies. Senior commanders and their staffs had to learn how to

■ *Below:* **The US policy of keeping units together throughout the war resulted in remarkable unit cohesion and maintained a high level of morale.**

translate Patton's aggressive theories into practical and workable tactics and command procedures. This process was eased considerably when Patton sacked many of the existing senior staff officers in the Third Army head-quarters, and replaced them with trusted figures who had served him in North Africa and Sicily.

Equipment

When Patton's troops started arriving in Great Britain they found new tanks, artillery, halftracks, jeeps and other equipment waiting for them. They would soon go into action with some of the most modern American weapons available at that time.

The main battle tank issued to the Third Army was the M4 Sherman, which was available in two main versions. The basic M4 was armed with a 75mm cannon and powered by a Continental R-975 radial engine, giving a top speed of 38.4km/h (24mph). The up-armoured, up-gunned and up-powered M4A2 was the next most numerous tank in the Third Army, boasting a long-barrelled 76mm cannon and twin GM diesels, with a top speed of 48km/h (30mph). Specialist versions of the Sherman were available in large numbers, including a close-support version fitted with a 105mm howitzer to neutralize soft targets, such as infantry, trucks and anti-tank guns. There were also engineer and recovery versions, equipped with bulldozer blades and towing arms respectively.

These tanks were specially designed for the fast-moving type of armoured warfare envisaged by Patton. They were reliable and fuel-efficient, allowing them to drive between 160km (100 miles) and 192km (120 miles) on a full tank of fuel. The Sherman, however, was not designed for head-to-head combat with heavy German Panther and Tiger tanks. These monster tanks could easily

pick off a Sherman, even the up-armoured M4A2, at ranges in excess of 1000m (3280ft). At these ranges the American tank's guns stood little chance of penetrating the armour of their German opponents. Soon US tank crews had dubbed their Shermans "Ronsons", after the famous cigarette lighter, due to their habit of exploding when hit by German 75mm and 88mm shells.

To counter the German tank threat, US armoured units relied on their better radios to allow them to detect enemy tanks early, and then manoeuvre their own tanks to attack the vulnerable flanks of the German machines.

The main anti-tank weapons available to the Third Army were self-propelled tank destroyers, which were intended to be formed into highly mobile strike forces that would be massed to counter German tank attacks. Tank destroyers were basically Sherman chassis fitted with an open turret and armed with high-velocity cannons. Two versions were in service with the Third Army, the M10 Wolverine, which boasted a 76.2mm cannon, and the 76mm-armed M18 Hellcat.

Armoured cars and halftracks

Reconnaissance units of the Third Army were equipped with a number of wheeled and tracked light armoured vehicles. The M5 light tank with its 37mm cannon was the main tracked scout vehicle. It was often combined with M8 Greyhound armoured cars and GMC M3 armoured halftracks, providing transport for dismounted scout teams and armoured infantry squads. These vehicles were rugged and reliable, but the M3 halftrack lacked overhead protection from artillery shell splinters. The bulk of Patton's infantry-men rode in two-and-a-half-ton trucks, the "deuce-and-a-half", and dismounted just out of enemy small-arms range before moving into attack.

■ *Above* The 105mm M2A1 howitzer provided the majority of the heavy indirect fire support for the Third Army.

The heavy firepower of the Third Army was provided by its artillery. US infantry divisions boasted a mix of M2A1 105mm and M1 "Long Tom" 155mm howitzers. Some units also used 4.5in and M1917/18 155mm howitzers. The 105mm could fire out to 12.5km (7.8 miles), while the heavier 155mm could hit targets out to 20km (12.5 miles). Unlike the German Army, which relied on horses to tow its field guns, the US artillery branch was fully motorized and generally could keep up with advancing spearheads. Heavy fire support was available from 8in and 240mm howitzers, but these monsters were often left far behind when Patton's tanks were pushing deep behind enemy lines. Mobile fire support for armoured spearheads was provided by self-propelled howitzers mounted on tank and halftrack chassis. Light 75mm howitzers were installed on GMC M3 halftracks and M5 light tank chassis. Heavy mobile firepower was provided by the M7 self-propelled gun, which

was a M3 tank chassis converted to carry a 105mm howitzer. To direct the US artillery onto targets, observer officers had the use of Piper L-4 Cub or "Flying Grasshopper" scout planes to fly them over battle zones.

Patton's infantry were heavily armed with a wide range of weapons, including small arms, machine guns, mortars and anti-tank rockets. The main weapon of the US infantry was the M1 Garand rifle, supported by the magazine-fed Browning Automatic Rifle (BAR). Heavier firepower was provided by belt-fed .30in and .50in Browning machine guns. Indirect short-range firepower was provided by M2 60mm and M1 81mm mortars. The latter type of weapon could be mounted on M3 halftracks to give them mobility. Short-range defence against German panzers was provided

by M9 Bazooka anti-tank rocket launchers, which could penetrate and knock out a Panther or Tiger up to a range of 100m (328ft) range, though by armoured warfare standards this was often a little too close for comfort.

To keep the Third Army moving its engineers had a range of bridging equipment, enabling even the widest river to be spanned in a matter of hours. These included box girder bridges, treadmill, pontoon and float bridges and Bailey-type bridges. All these bridges could be carried on trucks to allow them to keep up with armoured spearheads. Bulldozers and other engineer vehicles were often needed to prepare bridging launch sites and to keep open road routes to them.

A key part of Patton's combat force were the fighter-bomber aircraft of XIX

■ *Above:* **A US M26 Pershing tank crosses a pontoon bridge over the Rhine in early 1945. Combat engineers were always in high demand to construct bridges over the many rivers traversing France and Germany.**

■ *Right:* The upgraded M4A2 Sherman was the second most common tank in the Third Army. It had a long-barrelled 76mm gun, thicker armour and a higher top speed.

■ *Right:* The standard armoured weapon of the Third Army was the M4 Sherman. It was outgunned by its German counterparts.

Tactical Air Command. Ground-attack aircraft included the excellent Republic P-47 Thunderbolt, armed with .50in machine guns and 500lb or 1000lb bombs. More potent was the North American P-51 Mustang, armed with machine guns, 500lb or 1000lb bombs and up to six 127mm rockets. These aircraft used armour-piercing .50in ammunition to allow them to punch through the thin roof armour of German tanks. For added terror effect, US fighter-bombers also regularly made use of napalm to engulf enemy troops in burning fuel. Reconnaissance versions of the Mustang were also available to provide detailed aerial photographs of the lie of the land ahead of Patton's armoured spearheads.

The US Army provided Patton with two main types of division for his campaign in France: armoured and infantry. Armoured divisions were designed for rapid exploitation of breakthroughs and then hot pursuit of a defeated enemy. The job of opening a breach in the enemy's frontline defences was left to the infantry divisions. An armoured division had a full strength of some 11,000 men, and boasted 186 M4 Sherman medium tanks and 77 M5 light tanks, 54 105mm self-propelled howitzers, more than 500 M3 armoured halftracks and some 2600 other vehicles.

Armoured divisions were usually commanded by a major-general, and they had a team of experienced officers to command the division's six manoeuvre battalions. The division had three combat commands, each led by a full "bird" colonel, to control a mix of armour and infantry battalions assigned for specific missions. Combat Command A (CCA) and Combat Command B (CCB) were the principal strike forces of the division, while the Combat Command Reserve (CCR) looked after troops resting from action or being prepared for combat. In support was the artillery command (Divarty) and the Trains Command that controlled the logistic assets of the division.

Armoured divisions had three armoured and three armoured infantry battalions assigned. The armoured battalions usually sported three medium companies each with 17 M4 Shermans and a light company with 17 M5s. The armoured infantry battalions were built around three companies and had some 1000 men. Each 12-man squad rode into battle in an M3 halftrack. Support elements were also mounted on specialized versions of the M3 halftrack.

Within a combat command, it was common for tank and infantry sub-

■ *Below:* The M10 Wolverine tank destroyer was the main anti-tank defence in Patton's army. It boasted a 76mm high-velocity gun.

■ *Above:* The M8 Greyhound provided the armoured reconnaissance element of the Third Army. It was often combined with the M3 halftrack (seen in the distance).

units to be swapped around between manoeuvre battalions to allow different tactical challenges to be overcome. Artillery, engineer, cavalry and other specialist troops could also be attached as needed.

This process was known as creating combined-arms teams. "Tank-heavy teams" were used where rapid movement was required or when enemy tanks were expected to be engaged. These usually involved the attachment of an armoured infantry company to a tank battalion. "Infantry-heavy teams" comprised a majority of infantry companies; they were used for attacks on towns and woods and during river-crossings. In each case the predominant arm would provide the command element of the team.

It was also possible to form a single super-battalion by merging a tank and an armoured infantry battalion into a single unit, usually under a dual-captaincy arrangement.

Patton trained his divisions to be expert in rapidly regrouping their combat commands to meet changing tactical situations. Drills and procedures were designed to accomplish this with as little fuss as possible. This was the key to the Third Army maintaining the momentum of its advance, and ensured that the Germans did not have time to re-establish their defences.

In the European theatre, US armoured divisions usually conducted two main types of offensive operations, known as the "Rat Race" and the "Slugging Match". The former was basically an advance to contact over open terrain in the face of minimal resistance. Tanks and armoured infantry

YOU ARE NOW
CROSSING THE
RHINE RIVER
THROUGH COURTESY
OF E CO. 17 ARMD.
ENGR. BN. AND
C CO. 202
ENGR. C. BN.

would intermingle, and when resistance was encountered, it was either crushed with a rapid charge or bypassed. The "Slugging Match" was a more deliberate operation against a known enemy position, in which the combat commands attacked in close cooperation to provide mutual support. Maximum use was made of artillery and air support according to a carefully choreographed plan.

Infantry divisions

US infantry divisions were numerically stronger than their armoured counterparts, with some 14,250 men under arms. Their structure was far less flexible than armoured divisions and was built around three infantry regiments, each of three battalions comprising 871 men. The regiments were able to mix and match the troops under their command in three battalion-sized combat teams.

Although the infantry fought on foot, they did possess operational and strategic mobility from the 2000 vehicles assigned to each infantry division. These trucks could lift a full infantry regiment at a time, though a shuttle needed to be established to move all the division's combat infantry during long-distance moves. This meant Patton's infantry divisions could generally keep up with his tank units on the race through France, although they needed tank support if they encountered heavy resistance.

For specific operations, such as set-piece assaults or to deal with German counterattacks, it was common for infantry divisions to be assigned independent tank, tank destroyer, heavy artillery and mechanized reconnaissance battalions from a pool held as a Third

■ *Left:* **The engineer regiments of the Third Army became adept at deploying bridges. Their expertise allowed Patton's armour to thrust forward at great speed.**

Army reserve. This system, however, had many drawbacks because it meant infantry and tank units were often unused to working together, unlike the elements of armoured divisions.

One area where the Third Army excelled was in air-to-ground cooperation. XIX Tactical Air Command provided every combat command with a small radio team working in a radio-equipped jeep or tank so they could keep up with the armoured division's spearhead. A number of roving teams were also available to work with infantry divisions or cavalry scout groups. These tactical air liaison officers (TALO) were the eyes and ears of the US fighter-bombers, reporting the position of friendly troops and assigning targets for attack. In emergencies the US Army allowed ground troops to call down air support, and tank commanders were trained to talk to pilots on their radios.

Patton demanded that his advancing armoured column have dedicated air cover throughout the hours of daylight. In rotation, squadrons of fighter-

bombers were assigned to each combat command as it advanced. The TALO would work with his ground commander to assign targets to be attacked. At the same time, other fighter-bombers would be ordered to fly ahead of tank columns, neutralizing enemy resistance along the line of advance. XIX Tactical Air Command split its sorties almost equally between close air support for troops in contact with the enemy (42 percent) and interdiction missions deep behind German lines (40 percent), unlike its United States Army Air Force (USAAF) and Royal Air Force (RAF) counterparts who only allocated around a quarter of their missions to close air support. Patton insisted that support for his spearheads receive maximum effort.

"I'd have fighter-bombers out in front [of Patton's tanks] and we'd try to take care of anything out there," recalled Otto Weyland. "But sometimes there'd be concealed stuff. So then they'd yell. I'd have an air liaison officer in the lead tank who communicated with the

■ *Above:* An M3 halftrack mounting a heavy gun in action against Axis positions in Tunisia. The halftrack was an extremely versatile military vehicle.

fighter group that was working up front somewhere. Whistle them back and they'd be there in three minutes. Wham! Wham! Wham! They'd keep rolling."

In June 1944 Patton's army was built around four army corps, which were assigned the command of individual divisions for specific operations. Each corps was commanded by a senior major-general who put his personal stamp on how he operated his corps. Each corps had its own specialist reconnaissance, artillery, anti-aircraft, tank destroyer, military police, engineer, quartermaster and communications units to allow it to operate as a self-contained force. Two or three field artillery groups equipped with around 50 155mm heavy artillery pieces were the corps commander's prize asset, and his corps artillery headquarters was used

to concentrate the fire of these guns on decisive targets. A cavalry reconnaissance group also acted as the corps commander's eyes and ears in fast-moving battles. The firepower of each corps, in turn, could be augmented by specialist units controlled by the Third Army, which in August 1944 included the 2nd and 15th Cavalry Groups, 1st Tank Destroyer Brigade and a number of specialist engineer groups.

For the Normandy campaign, Patton was given VIII, XII, XV and XX Corps, but at various points over the course of his advance through France he would have to transfer some of his corps to other armies. These corps headquarters had all yet to see action, but many of the senior officers were highly experienced.

VIII Corps was under the command of Major-General Troy H. Middleton,

■ *Below:* US troops try to dig their truck out of the mud. With thousands of vehicles using the same routes, heavy rain could turn country roads into mudbaths.

whom Patton described as "one of the easiest Corps Commanders to do business with … and also one of the most efficient". A veteran of World War I, Middleton commanded divisions in Sicily and Italy with some success and he had a reputation for calmness under fire. While not as outwardly charismatic as Patton, he could be an aggressive commander and proved himself to be very daring during the advance into Brittany. Middleton's troops were the first element of the Third Army to see action, deploying to Normandy in mid-June to participate in the advance on Cherbourg as part of Lieutenant-General Omar Bradley's First Army. They switched to Patton's command on the eve of his breakout operation.

XII Corps had two commanders during the French campaign, after Major-General Gilbert R. Cook was

■ *Above:* **A US 60mm mortar. This weapon was operated by a team of five men, and had a range of up to 1700m (5700ft).**

relieved early in August 1944 due to ill health. "Doc" Cook was described as an "audacious leader" by Patton, but he had to be hospitalized a few days after the breakout with circulation problems in his legs.

"Matt" Eddy

The new XII Corps commander was Major-General Manton S. Eddy, who had a reputation for being hyperactive and highly stressed. He had successfully led the 9th Infantry Division during the assault on the port of Cherbourg, after commanding it in action in North Africa and Sicily. Although Patton was normally suspicious of plump, over-weight officers, Patton grew to like "Matt" Eddy because of his aggressive mania for mobility. His headquarters and divisions hardly ever halted for more than a few hours at a time, before Eddy would drive them forward. He was also expert at exploiting minor successes and then pushing more troops forward to capitalize on his gains. Like Patton, he loved to stage impromptu medal ceremonies to reward his troops' heroism, and was often to be seen on the frontline with his troops. His enthusiasm could be dramatically turned around by minor setbacks, though, and he was always worrying about the vulnerability of his flanks during the advance across France, prompting Patton to constantly reassure him not to be concerned.

Major-General Wade H. Haislip, the commander of XV Corps, was a trusted subordinate of Patton, who had great confidence in him and his troops. He had a lot in common with Patton and shared a love of things French, after graduating from the French staff college. Patton was very impressed by Haislip, and fought hard to stop his corps being transferred from the Third Army in September 1944.

Patton's fourth corps commander, Major-General Walton H. Walker, was another World War I infantryman, but he had been selected to command one of the first armoured divisions to be formed in 1942 at the start of the expansion of the US Army. As XX Corps commander, "Johnnie" Walker had a reputation as an aggressive officer who would fight any time, any place, with anything that Patton desired to give him. His command became known as the "Ghost Corps" because of the speed of its advance.

XIX Tactical Air Command

The final major combat element of the Third Army was Brigadier-General Otto Weyland's XIX Tactical Air Command, although technically it had dual chain of command reporting to Lieutenant-General Lewis H. Brereton's Ninth US Army Air Force; which, in turn, was part of Air Chief Marshal Sir Trafford Leigh-Mallory's Allied Air Expeditionary Air Force.

At the peak of its strength in early August 1944, XIX Tactical Air Command boasted a paper strength of more than 600 combat aircraft, although on a given day only some 400 machines were ready for action. The command was split between two wings, the 110th and 303rd. It had seven fighter groups in all, five of which were each equipped with a paper strength of 75 P-47s, plus two groups with some 75 P-51s apiece.

XIX Tactical Air Command was forward-deployed to airstrips in the Normandy bridgehead, and as the Third Army moved forward it began establishing new airstrips to allow its fighters to give Patton's men the air cover they needed. Often Weyland's fighter groups out-ranged their supply lines and Douglas C-47 Dakota transports had to be pressed into service to fly fuel, spares and ordnance forward to temporary airfields.

During the advance across France the Third Army's strike force was made

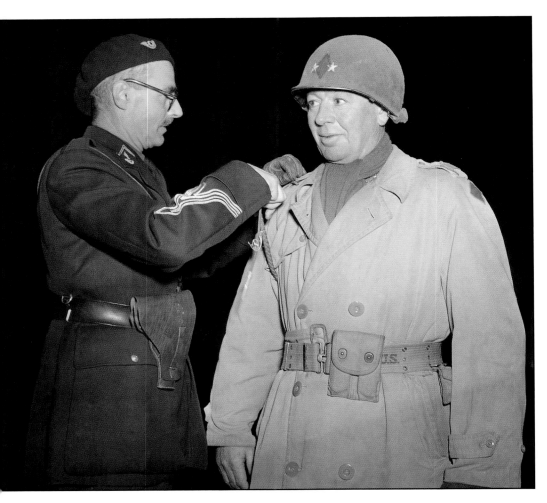

■ *Left:* Major-General S. LeRoy Irwin, the commanding officer of the 5th Infantry Division, is presented with France's premier order, the *Légion d'Honneur*, at Metz on 27 November 1944.

up of five armoured divisions, four US and one Free French. The most famous was the 4th Armored Division, or "Patton's Best", under the command of Major-General John S. Wood. "Tiger Jack", as he was known, was once described as "the Rommel of the American forces" because of his daring and dynamic command of his division. Wood's tactics were based on the German Blitzkrieg of 1940. His tanks moved fast, bypassing enemy resistance and keeping the Germans off guard. He took command of the 4th Armored in June 1942 and spent the next two years training his division to a peak of efficiency. This meant Wood and his officers were able to operate largely by very short verbal orders, allowing the

4th Armored to maintain the breakneck pace of its advance across France in July and August 1944. The division's officers were some of the best in the US Army, including Colonel Bruce Clarke, who moved on from leading the 4th Armored's Combat Command A to a top job in 7th Armored, and famously defended St. Vith during the Battle of the Bulge in December 1944. The division's 37th Tank Battalion was commanded with great flair by Lieutenant-Colonel Creighton Abrams, who later rose to be chief of staff of the US Army in 1972 (he died in 1974) and had the M1 main battle tank named after him, one of the greatest armoured vehicles of the late twentieth century. Patton commented, "I'm supposed to be

■ *Above:* A US soldier fires the M1918 Browning Automatic Rifle (BAR). It had an effective rate of fire of 550rpm, but only a 20-round magazine.

the best tank commander in the Army, but I have one peer – Abe Abrams." This was praise indeed.

Under Major-General Bob Grow, the 6th Armored Division grew to rival the 4th Armored as the Third Army's top tank outfit. Patton rated Grow as "one of the best armored force commanders the war produced", and he led the "Super Sixth" from 1942 through to the end of the war. Although not as flamboyant as Patton, Grow was

an expert at tank warfare, after serving in the US Army's experimental mechanized force in the 1930s. Grow and Wood were great rivals, and Patton delighted in playing them off against each other to spur them to advance faster and farther.

The 5th Armored Division was assigned to the Third Army during August 1944, and played a key part in the battle to close the Falaise Pocket, before being posted to the First Army.

Its commander, Major-General Lunsford E. Oliver, was a veteran of the North African campaign and a highly professional officer.

Major-General Lindsay M. Sylvester commanded the 7th Armored Division throughout the summer campaign in France as part of XX Corps. He was also a pre-war tank expert.

2nd Free French Armoured Division

The final armoured formation available to Patton was the 2nd Free French Armoured Division, which had been formed in England a year earlier to spearhead the liberation of its country from German occupation. A dashing French aristocrat, Vicomte Jacques-Philippe de Hautecloque, was placed in command by the Free French leader Charles de Gaulle, although he used a *nom de guerre*, Major-General Philippe Leclerc, to protect his family who remained in occupied territory.

Elite units of the Free French forces in Africa, Italy, the Middle East and England were drafted to the new division, which was outfitted with new American arms and equipment. The division was organized along the lines of US Army formations and trained in American tactics.

Leclerc had a fiery relationship with Patton, although the American's fluency in French helped smooth matters. Patton at one point called Leclerc "a baby" when he was sulking about orders he disagreed with, but the Frenchman's military professionalism usually won through. Relations become particularly strained during the run-up to the liberation of Paris, when de Gaulle demanded that Leclerc's troops receive the honour of being the first Allied troops to enter the French capital.

Following up behind the armoured spearheads of the Third Army were eight infantry divisions that bore the brunt of set-piece battles or mopping up

pockets of German resistance. The 35th Infantry Division, under Major-General Paul W. Baade, for example, was bloodied after landing in the first days after D-Day and had taken considerable casualties during the fighting in the Bocage country, before passing to Third Army command.

Patton's divisional commanders, Major-General S. LeRoy Irwin, 5th Infantry, Major-General Donald A. Stroh, 8th Infantry, Major-General Ira T. Wyche, 79th Infantry, Major-General Horace L. McBride, 80th Infantry, and Major-General Robert C. Macon of the 83rd Infantry, were all solid and professional officers who could be relied upon to perform well in difficult operational circumstances.

The bulk of the Third Army infantry were "green" when they landed in Normandy, but quickly matured into seasoned combat veterans. This was not with plenty of gentle encouragement by Patton. On the whole he was against sacking officers and soldiers who did not perform well in combat. He preferred to encourage them to improve, usually with comments spiced with numerous expletives. During the race across France Patton sacked only one division commander, Major-General Eugene M. Landrum, of the 90th Infantry Division, who was replaced by Brigadier-General Raymond S. McLain after a bungled attack on 30 July 1944.

Deployment

During the spring of 1944 the Third Army's corps and divisions were billeted in Northern Ireland, Scotland and the northwest of England, with Patton's headquarters in Peover Camp, south of Knutsford in Cheshire. As the date of D-Day approached, Patton was told to prepare to move his troops towards the south of England, before embarking onto ships for the short voyage to the Normandy beachhead.

■ *Above:* US tankers point out the damage caused by a German round – a lucky escape for this Sherman crew.

Elements of VII Corps began to cross to France in mid-June, and late in the month Third Army Headquarters moved to Breamore, near Salisbury. Less than a week later, on 5 July, the Forward Echelon of Third Army Headquarters embarked on Landing Ship Tanks (LSTs) and began sailing for France. "Lucky Forward" was established at Nehou, south of Cherbourg, in time for Patton to take up residence on 6 July. The remainder of the Third Army followed over the next three weeks. Patton was ready to go to war.

CHAPTER 3

THE BATTLE FOR NORMANDY

"I have a horrible feeling that the fighting will be over before I ever get in, but I know this is not so, as destiny means me to be in [the war]."
Patton, diary entry on D-Day

In the early hours of 6 June 1944, Allied forces began to land on the northern coast of France to begin the liberation of Europe from Nazi tyranny.

After almost five years of global conflict, Adolf Hitler's Third Reich was in retreat. Nazi forces had been driven from North Africa, most of the western Soviet Union and southern Italy. For three years the Soviet leader, Josef Stalin, had been pressing the Western Allies, Great Britain and the United States of America, to open a "Second Front" in northwest Europe to engage and destroy the 60 German divisions guarding the so-called Atlantic Wall.

Fearful that if any invasion of Europe was defeated, the psychological and military damage to the Allied cause would be irreparable, Allied leaders held back ordering an invasion until their forces were fully prepared to take on Hitler's Wehrmacht. The invasion was postponed through 1943 and the Allies set late spring in 1944 as the target date for any cross-Channel amphibious assault. During the winter of 1943–44 more than two million men and massive quantities

■ *Left:* US troops come ashore at Normandy following the initial assaults. Though the Third Army was not detailed to take an active role in the D-Day landings, it played a pivotal part in breaking out from the Normandy beachhead.

of war material had been massed in Great Britain, ready for Operation Overlord. The Allies were gambling all – the invasion could not fail.

To lead this immense and risky endeavour, the Allies drafted in their best generals, admirals and air marshals, who soon set to work crafting a complex plan for the invasion. Leading this effort was the US Army's General Dwight D. Eisenhower or, as he was popularly known, "Ike", who was designated the Supreme Allied Commander of the Supreme Headquarters Allied Expeditionary Force (SHAEF) in December 1943. From his London headquarters, Eisenhower began to gather around him his team for the coming invasion, and he soon turned to the British Army's General Bernard

Montgomery to review the progress of planning to date.

"Monty" was far from impressed by what he found. His experience in Sicily and Italy made him think the plan for a landing on a narrow bridgehead in Normandy was foolish, and he called for an assault by five divisions on a broad front. Once a bridgehead was firmly established, armoured divisions would strike out to capture major ports to allow more than two million men, including Patton's Third Army, and their material to flow into France, enabling the Allies to take on and defeat the German Army in the west. Eisenhower and the American ground commander for the invasion, Lieutenant-General Omar Bradley, had also been uneasy about the original plan

■ **Above: Front row, from right to left, Field Marshal Voroshilov, Soviet premier Josef Stalin, chairman of the Supreme Soviet Mikhail Kalinin and Soviet foreign minister Vyacheslav Molotov. Stalin had continually pressed for the opening of the "Second Front" in the West.**

■ Above: The Allied supreme command for Operation Overlord. Seated, from left to right, Air Chief Marshal Tedder, General Eisenhower and General Montgomery. Standing, from left to right, General Bradley, Admiral Ramsay, Air Chief Marshal Leigh-Mallory and General Walter Bedell Smith.

and quickly saw the logic of Montgomery's argument. The plan for D-Day was recast. To keep the Germans guessing as to where the invasion would take place, a massive deception operation, codenamed Fortitude, was set up to make them think the Allies would land in the Pas-de-Calais, on the opposite side of the Straits of Dover. This was the shortest sea distance from England, but contained the heaviest concentration of German defences, which the Allies wished to avoid at all cost. Patton played a big part in Fortitude, being portrayed in the media as commander of Army Group Patton based in southeast England, to make the Germans think he was poised to lead the Allied invasion force into northwest France. The Germans were convinced that Patton, as

the most aggressive Allied general, would lead the invasion, and they easily fell for the Fortitude deception.

Over the coming months, the complex plans for the world's largest-ever amphibious landing were rewritten, as troops were trained, weapons tested, ships positioned, aircraft prepared and missions rehearsed – time and time again. Nothing was left to chance.

Waiting for the Allies in Hitler's Fortress Europe were almost a million German fighting men, manning the huge Atlantic Wall or poised behind it to counterattack any invasion.

Hitler loved to order the pouring of thousands of tons of concrete into the many defensive lines built by Organization Todt construction engineers during the war. The mere act of creating

huge "facts on the ground" gave him a warm feeling. Concrete bunkers could not retreat during the mobile battles his generals were so keen on. Not surprisingly, the Führer had great hopes for his Atlantic Wall. Once the Allied invaders were trapped on France's beaches by the mines, booby-traps and machine-gun posts of the Atlantic Wall,

he would order his carefully nurtured panzer reserves to finish them off. That, at least, was the theory.

The reality was less impressive. Few of the 60 infantry divisions garrisoning the Atlantic Wall were top-rate units; the majority were made up of former Russian prisoners of war or medically substandard Germans. Away from the

■ *Above:* The Atlantic Wall was a series of massive concrete structures with pillboxes and gun emplacements. It was supplemented by minefields.

Russia. The arrival at the end of 1943 of Field Marshal Erwin Rommel, the famous Desert Fox, as commander of the invasion defences shook much of the complacency out of the German forces in France, but he was far from finishing his work when the Allies finally launched Operation Overlord.

German disagreements

Rommel and his boss disagreed on how to defeat the coming Allied invasion. Field Marshal Gerd von Rundstedt, Commander-in-Chief West, wanted to hold back the panzer reserves until the main landing beaches had been identified, and then he wanted to destroy them with a concentrated panzer counteroffensive. Fearing Allied airpower would devastate the panzers as they moved in for the kill, Rommel wanted to deploy the German armour close to the coast ready for instant counterattacks to throw the British and Americans back into the sea before they could get firmly established ashore. In his East Prussian bunker, Hitler could not make up his mind about what to do. In the end he made the worst of all possible decisions: to move a couple of divisions close to the coast in Normandy, insisting nonetheless that they were not to move without his personal approval. This was the start of Hitler's micro-management of the Battle

■ *Above right:* The German tank ace Field Marshal Erwin Rommel (centre) inspects part of the Atlantic Wall in mid-1944.

coast, the 10 panzer and panzer-grenadier divisions held in reserve were also of mixed quality. Many were in the process of being rebuilt after suffering heavy losses on the Eastern Front. There was also a question mark over the leadership of German armies in France, which was seen as a comfortable backwater, far away from the horrors of

■ *Above:* British
and American
troops aboard
landing craft
stream towards
the Normandy
coastline on D-Day.

for Normandy that would eventually prove so disastrous.

After a day-long delay due to bad weather, Eisenhower ordered the invasion to begin on 6 June 1944. The assault force was immense: 50,000 men were scheduled to land on the first day of the invasion alone. Another 34 divisions were poised in Great Britain to pour ashore in the three months following D-Day. More than 4000 landing craft and assault vessels carried the first wave of troops to the beaches, supported by some 800 merchant vessels, 138 major warships, 1000 minesweepers and 300 smaller craft. Overhead some 11,000 aircraft were in action bombing German positions and lines of communications or dropping paratroopers to protect the flanks of the bridgehead. Inland more than 100,000 members of the French Resistance were acting on codewords broadcast by the British Broadcasting Corporation (BBC) to begin sabotage attacks against the German occupiers.

On four of the five invasion beaches, the attackers easily overwhelmed the German defenders with minimal casualties and were soon pressing inland. The US troops heading for Omaha Beach, however, ran into stiff resistance and suffered more than 1500 dead before consolidating their toehold on the European mainland. Overall Allied casualties on D-Day were in the region of 11,000, of which only some 2500 were fatalities. The gamble had paid off.

The German reaction to D-Day was far from sure-footed. Many key commanders, including Rommel, were away from their headquarters on 6 June.

■ *Above:* US troops killed during the initial D-Day assault lie covered on the beach. The Third Army was fortunate that it did not have to suffer the trauma of the landings.

■ *Right:* A German soldier lies dead outside the pillbox he was manning, overlooking the US landing zone at Utah Beach.

Counterattacks by the troops in Normandy were half-hearted, and Hitler delayed releasing the panzer reserves because of continuing fears of another landing in the Pas-de-Calais. It was not until 7 June that the first significant counterattack got under way, when the Waffen-SS *Hitlerjugend* Division slammed into the Canadians north of Caen.

British and Canadian troops came ashore on the eastern flank of the Allied invasion. Their objective was to swiftly capture Caen and then push armoured divisions inland to complete the German rout. Rommel had other ideas.

For the next six weeks, Montgomery launched the British and Canadian troops forward in a series of set-piece battles of growing intensity, as more forces poured into the bridgehead and

became available for action. First he sent forward the 7th Armoured Division – the famous Desert Rats – on a daring outflanking attack to the west of Caen. German Tiger tanks ambushed the force

■ *Left:* US fighter-bombers, such as these P-47 Thunderbolts, were crucial in driving back German counterattacks and disrupting enemy movements in Normandy. The relationship between armour and airpower was exceptionally fruitful during the Third Army's rampage across France.

and sent it reeling back to the bridgehead. Next, the British XXX and VIII Corps began Operation Epsom to envelop Caen, but four Waffen-SS panzer divisions concentrated to hammer them hard. Into July, Montgomery continued to chip away at the Germans until his infantry were at the gates of Caen.

To the west, the Germans were giving the Americans under Bradley a hard time in the difficult Bocage country. Rommel was desperate to prevent the Allies capturing the port of Cherbourg, which would considerably ease their logistic problems. The defence was led by veteran German parachute and Waffen-SS divisions, but there were nowhere near as many German tanks facing the Americans as the British.

During the first two months of the Battle for Normandy, all the Allied ground forces were under the command of Montgomery and his Twenty-First Army Group headquarters. Eisenhower was still back in England and had limited control over the unfolding battle. Monty's conduct of the early phases of the Normandy campaign is still very controversial, as rival Allied generals and their acolytes pushed to demonstrate their contribution to the eventual victory. At the heart of Allied strategy was the need to ensure the British and American alliance remained solid. This was Eisenhower's area of expertise, but some of his subordinates lacked his finesse at soothing egos and forging consensus.

By the end of June the Germans had massed some 10 panzer divisions in Normandy with more than 1500 tanks and armoured vehicles. Even though the British and Americans had more than

■ *Below:* A German Panzer IV tank of the *Hitlerjugend* SS Panzer Division with its crew. The female names seen in white were written by the young crew, and were probably the names of sweethearts back home in Germany.

double this number of tanks, an Allied breakthrough seemed elusive. The Soviets had also just begun a major offensive on the Eastern Front, which ripped the heart out of the German defences and cost the Wehrmacht a further 500,000 casualties. If the German line in Normandy could be breached, Hitler's Reich would never recover. The Allies had to strike soon.

To break this impasse, Montgomery proposed a new strategy. Rather than attempt a breakthrough along a broad front, the aim would now be for the British and Canadians to continue to pin the bulk of the German armour in the east around Caen to allow the Americans to break through on a narrow front in the west. Once through the German defences, US tanks would swing both west and east to capture the vital Brittany ports and ultimately to defeat the German forces facing the British and Canadians around Caen. Bradley liked the new plan, but fierce German resistance during the drive on Cherbourg meant that it took him longer than expected to develop his strategy and build up his forces, and thus as July wore on US casualties rose. And as the Americans tried to batter through the Bocage, there were some complaints that Montgomery was making GIs pay in blood for his pursuit of glory.

Patton was equally critical of Bradley's slowness to break through,

commenting, "Sometimes I get desperate over the future. Brad and [Courtney] Hodges [commander designate of First Army] are such nothings. Their virtue is that they get along by doing nothing. I could break through in three days if I commanded. They try and push all along the front and have power nowhere. All that is necessary now is to take more chances by leading them with armored divisions and covering their advances with air bursts. Such an attack would have to be made on a narrow sector, whereas at present we are trying to attack all along the line."

Bernard Montgomery then launched Operation Goodwood on 18 July in an attempt to outflank Caen from the east. Three British armoured divisions, with almost 900 tanks, backed up by 10,000 infantry, 700 guns and 2000 heavy bombers, were to smash through the weakened German lines and break into open country.

The Germans weathered the massive bombardment, and an improvised line of Tiger tanks and 88mm flak guns ripped the British attack force apart. Confusion reigned in the British ranks, and the attack stalled without breaching the German lines. Some 270 burning hulks of British tanks littered the battlefield. While the result was a tactical defeat for the British, it doomed the German defences in Normandy. Rommel's panzer reserves had to be committed to hold the line for the next crucial two weeks as the Americans gathered their strength to strike.

At almost the same time, Rommel was hospitalized after his staff car was strafed by British Typhoon fighter-bombers and a group of German officers planted a bomb in Hitler's East Prussian headquarters. The Führer escaped the explosion but emerged from the ruins of his map room even more convinced of the need to stop his generals retreating

■ *Above:* A knocked-out German tank lies smoking after being hit by Russian tank fire during the June 1944 Soviet offensive on the Eastern Front. Stalin had been pressing the Allies to open a "Second Front" to correspond with a fresh Russian drive, and in June 1944 he got his wish.

any more. Von Rundstedt had already resigned and his successor as Commander-in-Chief West, Field Marshal Günther von Kluge, now had even less freedom of manoeuvre. The defence of Normandy was being directed personally by the Führer.

The Bocage battle

Holding the German line opposite Bradley was Waffen-SS General Paul Hausser, who had been drafted in to lead the German Seventh Army after its commander, Colonel-General Friedrich Dollman, died of a heart attack at the end of June. Hausser was no Nazi automaton, but a cunning and determined commander with a reputation for being able to improvise skilfully in times of crisis. On the Eastern Front he had commanded the élite II SS Panzer Corps during the battles of Kharkov and Kursk in 1943, at times ignoring Hitler's questionable "fight to the last man and bullet" orders when he thought they threatened his troops with annihilation by Soviet encirclements.

Although he lacked the tank resources of Panzer Group West, later renamed Fifth Panzer Army, under Heinrich Eberbach, which was facing the British and Canadian armies, Hausser deployed his slender forces with great skill to maximize their capability to delay and confound the Americans. His troops turned every village and hedgerow into a fortress, defended by machine guns, mortars and anti-tank rockets. The Bocage terrain, with its impenetrable networks of sunken roads, thick hedges, dense woods and picturesque villages, was a nightmare to attack. American tanks and infantry could not manoeuvre around the German defences, but had to take each German strongpoint in a slow set-piece attack. Often before the Americans had consolidated their success, they were driven back by a snap German counterattack and had to begin the process all over again.

The first phases of Bradley's campaign in France were conducted in a methodical fashion that reflected his approach to battle. In the days after D-Day, the US Army had concentrated on joining up its two bridgeheads by capturing Carentan at the base of the Cotentin Peninsula on 12 June. Over the next two weeks Bradley concentrated on taking the port of Cherbourg, but by the time US troops had reached the city the key dockyards had been systematically demolished by the German defenders and put out of action.

A slow, bloody advance

While Bradley's troops were pushing north to Cherbourg, Rommel had a free hand to reinforce his defences opposite the American sector, pushing II Parachute Corps and LXXXIV Corps into the line opposite Bradley's men. The attack on Cherbourg exhausted the troops taking part, so the newly arrived VIII Corps under Troy Middleton was pushed into the line to help bolster the attempt to achieve a breakout to the south. The experience was very traumatic for the "green" GIs pushed into action for the first time during Bradley's new offensive.

VIII Corps attacked southwards on 3 July against the German LXXXIV Corps and immediately found itself bogged down in heavy fighting. The rate of advance was measured in yards and a high price was paid in blood. The 79th Infantry Division lost 2000 men in five days and Middleton's other divisions fared little better. In 12 days of fighting VIII Corps' butcher's bill had risen to 10,000 with little to show for it. Bradley threw VII Corps into the meat grinder on 4 July. It attacked across rain-sodden ground and lost 1400 men on the first day and 750 on the following day. Eleven days later, the corps had barely

moved the frontline more than 5km (3 miles) south, though had accrued 8000 casualties doing so.

On 7 July it was the turn of XIX Corps to advance, and Bradley assigned a tank division to it in the hope that it would open a way forward. The result was little better after the tanks became jammed in the narrow, hedge-lined roads and could not manoeuvre around the German strongpoints. In five days XIX Corps only managed to advance 10km (6 miles).

The only bright point for Bradley in this dismal period was the defeat of a counterattack by the German Panzer Lehr Division on 11 July, which was driven back with heavy losses.

Bradley was a methodical and determined man who picked himself up from these setbacks, and a new plan was

crafted to seize the town of St-Lô and defeat the German II Parachute Corps. After a massed artillery barrage, XIX and V Corps surged forward on 12 July in a pincer attack. In a six-day battle, Bradley fed three divisions into the contest against the battered remnants of the German 3rd Parachute and 352nd Infantry Divisions. The weight of firepower overwhelmed the German defences, and on 18 July American GIs entered St-Lô to find the town totally devastated. This victory cost Bradley another 6000 casualties, bringing his losses over the past 17 days to 40,000 men killed or wounded. His front had advanced less than 11km (7 miles). Many of Bradley's divisions were shattered by this bloody experience, with the long-suffering 90th Infantry Division recording 150 percent

■ *Above:* **Hitler (centre) was fortunate to survive the 20 July Bomb Plot. Following this, his acute paranoia led him to distrust his generals even more.**

■ *Above:* Moving up behind a hedge in the Bocage, three US troops fire on the enemy. The soldier on the far left is firing a fragmentation grenade from his rifle.

casualties among its frontline officers and 100 percent losses in its combat riflemen during the first six weeks of the Normandy campaign.

The one ray of sunshine was the fact that Hausser's battered divisions were in even worse shape than Bradley's troops. Unlike the American First Army, the German forces in Normandy had not received any significant reinforcement during July. Hitler's continued belief that another Allied landing was to be made in the Pas-de-Calais ensured that the Fifteenth Army, the last uncommitted German force in the West, was kept back from the Normandy Front. A massive Soviet breakthrough on the Eastern Front – Operation Bagration – meant the German armies had to fight on with the resources they had at hand. The divisions manning the Normandy front

boasted little more than a couple of thousand frontline troops to hold their positions. Ammunition and fuel were in short supply because of incessant Allied bombing of German lines of communication (even food had to be transported to frontline troops at night due to Allied air superiority). Hope certainly seemed to be in short supply among the Germans in Normandy.

Morale among Bradley's divisions was clearly shaken by its bruising battles. Something drastic needed to be done to break through the German lines. Even before his attacks were running out of steam around St-Lô, Bradley was planning a major push to achieve a decisive breakthrough. This was dubbed Operation Cobra. It was more than just another thrust through the Bocage. The firepower of 2500 heavy bombers and fighter aircraft was

■ *Far left:* Waffen-SS General Paul Hausser. He was a cunning and sophisticated commander, but ultimately unable to stem the tide of US armour.

■ *Near left:* General Günther von Kluge. He later became a field marshal, and took his own life after fearing Hitler suspected him of treason.

to be concentrated on a narrow section of front, and then six divisions, including two armoured units, were to roll over the debris of the German defences. The objective was the town of Avranches at the gateway to Brittany. After Bradley's tanks had reached this objective, Patton's Third Army would be fed into the battle to swing westwards and seize the vital Brittany ports. At the same time, Lieutenant-General Courtney Hodges would take over command of the First Army and swing eastwards to roll towards the River Seine and complete the defeat of the German forces in Normandy. At this stage, a deliberate breakthrough and methodical advance was envisaged, not a dramatic breakout. Only as the battle developed would senior Allied commanders see the potential to encircle and trap the German armies facing them if they acted decisively.

To oversee this vastly expanded American effort, Bradley would be elevated to command the Twelfth Army Group, in theory putting him on a par with Montgomery himself. Eisenhower, however, would not have his

headquarters fully established on the continent until late August, leaving Montgomery effectively in charge of the high-level conduct of the final stages of the Normandy campaign.

Bradley briefed his commanders on 12 July, and over the next 12 days the preparations for Cobra were put in place. A 9.6-square-kilometer (6-square-mile) section of the front to the west of St-Lô, along the road to Périers, was selected as the bombing target, and 24 July was set as the start date. The key frontline defences would be saturated by some 5080 tonnes (5000 tons) of high explosive, napalm and white phosphorus. The Allied air commanders were worried about the danger of hitting their own troops and they proposed a 2743m (9000ft) safety margin, but Bradley insisted on half this distance. To ease the margin of safety, high-flying heavy bombers would hit the southern fringe of the target box, leaving low-flying fighter-bombers to strike at targets nearer the American lines.

When Allied commanders found out about the 20 July Bomb Plot against

Hitler, they realized the urgency of launching Operation Cobra. For George Patton kicking his heels in his command post far behind the front, the tension was clearly too much and he charged into Bradley's command tent, demanding, "For God's sake Brad, you've got to get me into this fight before the war is over."

The first wave of bombers took off on the morning of 24 July, but soon the target was obscured by cloud leading to the raid being cancelled. Some 500 aircraft did not receive the recall message and dropped 700 bombs on the target area. Unfortunately many landed behind US lines, killing 25 and wounding 130 GIs. The raid alerted the Germans to the fact that a major attack was brewing and their retaliatory artillery bombardment of US staging areas caused heavy casualties and confusion among the assault units.

The following morning the Allied air forces returned in strength to do the job properly. More than 1500 B-17 and B-24 heavy bombers, supported by a further 380 medium bombers and 550 fighter-bombers, dropped 4216 tonnes (4150 tons) of bombs on the target box. The sheer weight of bombs threw up a huge cloud of debris that obscured the target and led the final wave of aircraft to miss their targets. More than 100 American soldiers were killed and 490 wounded in this attack.

However, the effect on the Germans was devastating, with over 1000 killed by the bombing alone. In the target zone itself, three battalion command posts were demolished and a regiment was wiped out. The brunt of the bombardment fell on the remnants of the Panzer Lehr Division. Its commander, the veteran Fritz Bayerlein, estimated that 70 percent of the troops in the target area were either killed, wounded, stunned or driven mad. As the surviving Germans emerged from their ruined command posts or bunkers, they were

■ *Below:* **The disposition of German and Allied forces on the eve of Operation Cobra.**

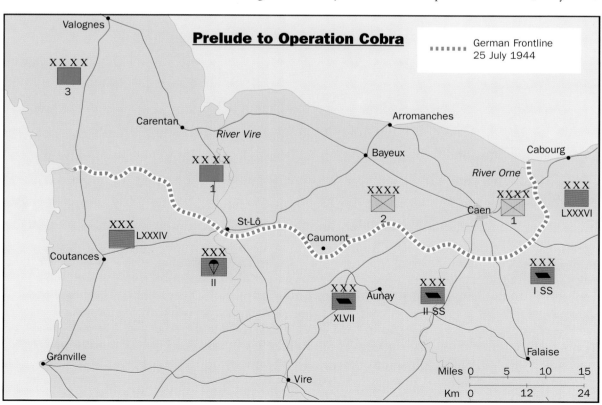

Prelude to Operation Cobra

German Frontline 25 July 1944

strafed by USAAF Thunderbolts and Mustangs, further adding to the confusion and panic among the demoralized defenders.

The bombing of the American frontlines had thrown the assault troops into some confusion, and it took time to get the first GIs to advance into the moonscape caused by the bombing. A handful of German machine-gun nests survived and slowed the American advance to a snail's pace. Bradley and his commanders were momentarily afraid the attack had failed. On the other side of the front, the Germans were also in crisis. Their lines were only holding together by a slender thread. There were no reserves left after Hausser sent his

■ *Above:* US troops with a destroyed enemy artillery piece after it was attacked by aircraft of XIX Tactical Air Command near Marigny.

last two battalions to bolster the threatened sector. They proved of little use after US fighter-bombers strafed them as they moved in daylight and decimated their column.

Fortunately the VII Corps commander, Major-General J. Lawton Collins, was made of sterner stuff and decided that he had to commit his two armoured divisions to crush German resistance once and for all. His lead tanks had been fitted with improvised hedge ploughs, called Rhinos, that allowed them to crush through the Bocage terrain and restore their freedom of manoeuvre. On the second day of the attack, "Lightning Joe" Collins' troops had all but rolled over the German defences. The Panzer Lehr Division was as good as annihilated and some 600 American tanks were heading south unopposed. On 28 July, Hausser threw his final card into the battle, pulling the 2nd SS *Das Reich* Panzer Division and 17th SS *Götz von Berlichingen* Panzergrenadier Division out of the front against VIII Corps and sending them in to hit Collins' columns in the flank. The result was a disaster, with the German panzer columns devastated by Allied airpower as they manoeuvred to intercept the American formations. A brief tank battle ensued that temporarily halted VII Corps, but the movement of the two Waffen-SS divisions completely unhinged the German defences in western Normandy.

VIII Corps strikes

Troy Middleton's VIII Corps had arrived in Normandy a month before as the advance guard of Patton's Third Army, only to find itself attached to Bradley's First Army for the vicious battles in the Bocage. His infantry divisions had certainly been blooded in those deadly duels with Hausser's Seventh Army, but he had yet to commit his armour.

Once Hausser moved his panzers eastwards to counter the American breakthrough, Middleton launched the 4th and 6th Armored Divisions forward. The weakened German line broke under the combined weight of some 300 Shermans rolling forward, and the remnants of three German infantry divisions were cut pieces. The road south was open. On 28 July the "Super Sixth" advanced south through Lessay and headed down the main road to Coutances. Five kilometers (three miles) to the east, the 4th Armored moved through Périers and also had Coutances in its sights. All that blocked their way was the debris of German columns that had been shot to pieces by Allied fighter-bombers. By the evening they were through Coutances and heading south towards Avranches. Combat Command B of the 4th Armored took Coutances in a flanking attack. In the wake of the American tanks came the 79th and 8th Infantry Divisions, who were following close on the heels of the 6th and 4th Armored Divisions, respectively.

During 28 July General Patton was summoned to Bradley's headquarters to be told that that in three days' time the Third Army would be activated and unleashed into Brittany. In the meantime, he would be given interim command of Middleton's troops so he could secure his jumping-off points around Avranches. Without hesitating, Patton drove down to Middleton's headquarters and put the latter in the picture about his intentions.

Early the next morning, Patton headed south to Coutances to get a feel for the battle and encourage his armoured spearheads forward. Quickly the troops of VIII Corps got to know what it meant to be under Patton's command. He found the 6th Armored halted at a river while their officers studied a map. Ignoring a group of German troops nearby, Patton strode into the river to test its depth. Finding it was not at all deep, Patton unleashed a torrent of expletives to get his tank crews moving. Patton's next target was a battalion of the 90th Infantry Division whom he found digging foxholes. "It is stupid to be afraid of a beaten enemy," he shouted at the cowering troops. Suitably invigorated with fighting spirit, Patton's spearheads spent 29 July motoring at full speed towards the town of Avranches.

The 6th Armored saw action for the first time that day, when Combat Command A, supported by its divisional artillery, forced a crossing of the River Sienne west of Coutances, by fording the shallow stream and scaling the bluffs beyond at twilight after clearing moderate resistance on the north bank. 6th Armored advanced 42km (26 miles) on its first day in combat. The divisional plan stipulated a development in two columns, with Combat Command A following Combat Command B across the river and then advancing on the left flank. During the following 48-hour period

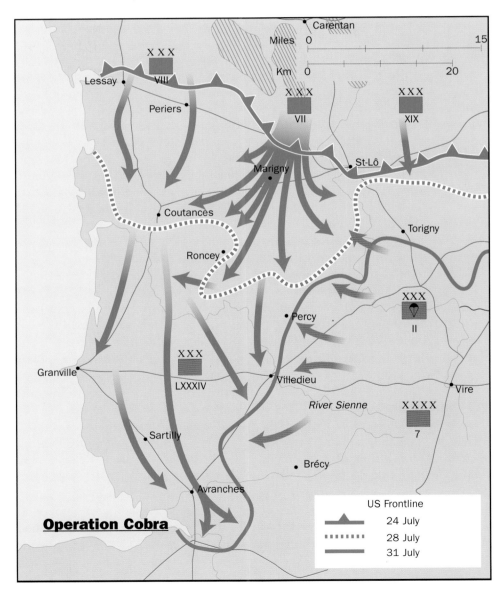

Left: **The progression of Operation Cobra as it advanced towards Avranches in July 1944.**

■ *Right:* US troops enter the French town of Coutances. The 4th Armored Division's Combat Command B had taken the town on 29 July.

the division swept along the Atlantic coast. The city of Granville was not defended, but Bréhal was surrounded by many strongpoints. More than 800 prisoners were captured during the division's advance.

Corporal Albert O. Maranda, who served in the 4th Armored Division's 94th Armored Field-Artillery Battalion, was in the vanguard of the advance and recorded the frantic events in his diary:

"29th July: Raining – moved out at 07:28 hours. Went down St-Lô–Périers highway through Périers. All towns and villages in shambles. Périers almost flattened – people streaming back to their former homes if they can find them. Bivouacked about [10 kilometers] six miles outside of St-Sauveur Lendelin. Here we go again, moved into new bivouac area [six and a half kilometers] four miles north of Coutances. We are taking nearly 1000 prisoners a day. We lost a halftrack, the men missing. General

Wood led the attack personally. 30th July: Battalion is the spearhead of drive south. Traffic is pretty heavy. We moved out at 08:25 hours travelling south through Coutances, most of city is destroyed. We bivouacked about [five kilometers] three miles north of Cérences. Ate then moved out and bivouacked again. Jerries shelled our position, moved out. Used T5 [halftrack] to rout out some Jerries, who wouldn't come out. I got one with my machine gun. He was trying to circle us. Moved back in old position. Bivouacked six and a half kilometers (four miles) up road. Infantry flushing out hedgerows on either side of us. Haven't had a chance to shave for three days. Got five hours' sleep finally – still eating K rations."

The German front was collapsing all around Hausser. He himself had to dodge past an American tank to get back to his headquarters. However, that too was soon surrounded by US troops.

To the west the remnants of the German LXXXIV Corps, including the two Waffen-SS panzer divisions, were trapped between VIII and VII Corps at Roucy. Hausser made his own escape during the night and ordered his trapped troops to break out to the west. They managed to fight their way past the American columns in the darkness, but left 4000 prisoners and hundreds of burnt-out vehicles behind them.

In front of Patton's spearhead was nothing but confused and defeated German units fleeing for their lives. XIX Tactical Air Command's fighter-bombers roamed ahead of the American columns strafing any German traffic they could find. The biggest problem

■ *Above:* US tanks and infantry in jeeps advance down a road near Coutances. Most of the buildings have been destroyed by artillery fire.

for 4th Armored was what to do with all the prisoners it was taking. In the end they were simply disarmed and ordered to march north on their own to find a prisoner-of-war camp. On the evening of 30 July, the 4th Armored's Combat Command B rolled into Avranches and found the town deserted of Germans. However, it was soon attacked from the north by a column of several hundred German troops who had been bypassed in the retreat. After a brief firefight the Germans surrendered, but when another group of Germans attacked, the prisoners escaped from the tank company guarding the northern approaches to the town.

Rounding up prisoners

A large group of Germans managed to escape westwards through Avranches during the night, but with daylight US fighter-bombers appeared and ensured the 4th Armored remained firmly in control of the town. A series of mopping-up attacks rounded up hundreds of Germans scattered around Avranches. During 31 July, fighter-bomber pilots returning from patrol reported that the key bridge over the River Sélune at Pontaubault was undefended, and thus John Wood ordered an immediate attack to seize this golden opportunity.

The Germans, realizing the danger to their position in Brittany, had dispatched a battalion, backed up by assault guns, to secure the bridge before the Americans could get to it. Wood's men were quicker. After his Shermans rolled over the bridge they turned southeast to confront the approaching German column. After a brisk exchange of fire, the outgunned Germans beat a hasty retreat to St-Malo. During the day the 4th and 6th Armored Divisions captured 4000 prisoners between them and the follow-up infantry bagged another 3000 Germans. This was a significant part of the 20,000 captured during the six days of Operation Cobra. In four days of breakneck advance VIII Corps' total casualties amounted to only 700 killed and wounded. It was a far cry from the Bocage fighting.

Advance to glory

That evening Patton gathered his staff in the "Lucky Forward" command post to announce that they would assume full operational control of VIII Corps tomorrow, ready for the advance into Brittany. The role of the Third Army would, however, remain secret from the world to maintain the fiction that Patton was still waiting in southeast England to lead the invasion of the Pas-de-Calais and thus distract the German Fifteenth Army from the Normandy Front. He was in a feisty mood, and concluded his speech in true George Patton fashion.

"There's another thing I want you to remember. Forget this goddamn business of worrying about our flanks, but not to the extent we don't do anything else. Some goddamn fool once said that flanks must be secured and since then sons-of-bitches all over the world have been going crazy guarding their flanks. We don't want any of that in the Third Army. Flanks are something for the enemy to worry about, not us. I don't want to get any messages saying that, 'We are holding our positions'. We're not holding anything! Let the Hun do that. We are advancing constantly and we're not interested in holding on to anything except the enemy. We're going to hold on to him by the nose and we're going to kick him in the ass; we're going to kick the hell out of him all the time and we're going to go through him like crap through a goose. We have one motto; *L'audace, l'audace, toujours l'audace!* [Daring, daring, always daring!] Remember that gentlemen."

CHAPTER 4

DRIVE TO BRITTANY AND LE MANS

"The waiting was pretty bad … but now we are in the biggest battle I have ever fought and it is going fine, except for at one town we have failed to take. I am going there in a minute to kick someone's ass."

Patton, early August 1944.

A t noon on 1 August, Patton's Third Army was declared operational and took control of the breakout from Avranches. Spearheading the advance into Brittany was Troy Middleton's VIII Corps, while just behind was Wade Haislip's XV Corps, which was to swing east and head for Le Mans. For the next week, Patton drove his troops forward at a relentless pace and ultimately kicked away the foundations of the German front in Normandy.

The main effort of the Third Army was initially to be the push into Brittany in line with the long-standing requirement to capture the deep-water ports of Brest and Lorient, as well as the town of Quiberon where US Army engineers planned to build a new port. This was considered essential by Allied planners who were worried about how to supply their huge

■ *Left:* An American Sherman tank advances past wrecked German equipment and dead horses on the road to Avranches during the US drive to Brest. Whereas the US Army was fully motorized, the German Army relied on horse-drawn artillery.

armies for a long, deliberate campaign to drive the Germans from France. Patton, however, had greater ambitions and had already seen the war-winning potential of swinging the majority of his army eastwards to encircle the bulk of German forces fighting the British and Canadians at Caen. However, this plan had yet to be officially adopted by Montgomery and Eisenhower, so Patton did not yet have permission to change the direction of his advance.

Patton was not, however, about to charge into battle of his own accord. After his disgrace in Sicily, where he was accused of slapping a soldier, and the media outcry over a speech he made on 25 April 1944 at Knutsford, where his comment, ". . . it is the evident destiny of the British and Americans, and, of course, the Russians, to rule the world", appeared to insult the Russians by almost forgetting their importance as an ally, Patton did not feel this was the time to start disobeying orders. He kept his counsel but ordered his staff to prepare contingency plans. Patton felt, however, that he could hasten the moment when his superior would have to let him have his head, if he could manoeuvre into position to quickly execute an out-flanking attack to the east. So on the afternoon of 1 August, he descended on Avranches to do the impossible: move two armoured and two infantry divisions, with more than 100,000 men and 20,000 vehicles, across a single bridge in a one-street town in two days. He readily admitted that if he had proposed the idea at the US Army staff

■ *Above* **On the road to Avranches. Since the US Army Air Corps had control of the skies, all usual vehicle interval discipline was cast aside in the rush to exploit the breakout.**

college at Leavenworth he would have failed his exams. This was not strategy – it was traffic control.

Task Force A, a 3500-strong mobile force, moved through Avranches during the night of 1 August, and by the afternoon the 4th Armored Division was motoring south from Avranches towards Rennes. It had the mission of pushing through the town to the Bay of Biscay and cutting the Brittany peninsula off from the rest of France. Meanwhile, back in Avranches chaos reigned as convoys from different US divisions got jammed in the town's tight streets and the single bridge over the River Sélune was totally grid-locked. The Third Army was a sitting duck for German air attacks.

Patton – traffic warden

When Patton arrived at the town he immediately took control of the situation in the only way he knew how, by elbowing a military policeman off a traffic-control box and taking over. For several hours, he stood in the centre of the traffic jam directing convoys, saluting cheering troops and "chewing out" lost or aimless officers. By the end of the day, Patton handed over his post in Avranches to senior officers from Haislip's corps and returned to directing his army. His intervention was dramatic. The 90th Infantry Division was through Avranches and heading southeast, while four divisions and a special task force were moving into Brittany.

The situation was worse for follow-up units of XV Corps, which became intermingled with elements of the First Army crossing the road south in an east-west direction. The 5th Armored Division history records the scene:

"Late that afternoon, when the traffic snarl was its worst, General Patton called a meeting of those divisional commanders who could be assembled quickly. The tension was extremely high. Everyone knew that if enemy bombers discovered this knot of men and vehicles jammed up around St-Denis, a severe blow could be struck against the advance. General Oliver and the other divisional commanders wondered if their heads might roll because of this tie-up. General Patton strode into the anxious gathering and opened the meeting. 'Gentlemen,' he said, 'we are in a hell of a mess, and it's all my fault.'

"Then he explained that in his haste to send the units south he had given orders directly to the division commanders without informing his staff. 'Now we shall just sit here until my staff can work out schedules and routes,' he declared. 'Then we shall continue.' The night was also filled with the rushing roar of artillery shells belched out by both the German and American batteries. Enemy bombers, hovering over part of the route, dropped flares and then followed these with bombs. When a segment of a column became separated from its lead elements, tank and halftrack commanders were able to decide in which direction to go at each fork or crossroads only by getting down on their hands and knees in the road and with their flashlights seeing which way the tracks led. But despite the congestion and confusion and the fact that this was their first night of real combat, Combat Command A and Combat Command B had arrived by dawn at their originally designated areas near St-George and St-Hilaire-du-Harcouët, south of the Sélune River."

The plan for Brittany

For Middleton, adjusting to Patton's style of command was difficult. The bruising experience in the Bocage fighting the previous month under Bradley had led Middleton and his staff to operate in a cautious and methodical way, with modest objectives and closely

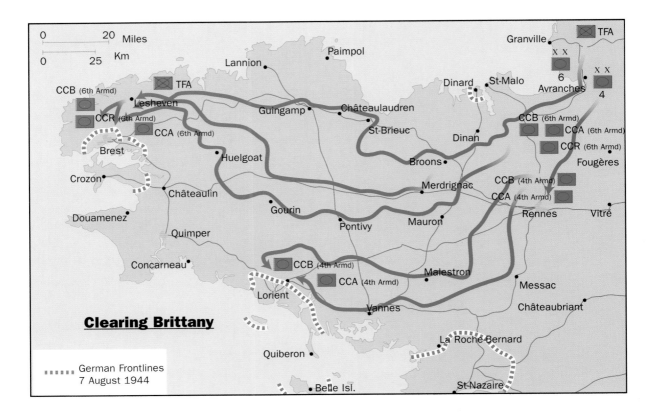

Clearing Brittany

```
...... German Frontlines
       7 August 1944
```

guarded flanks. Advances were then calculated in a few hundred yards a day. Patton was thinking in terms of advancing dozens of miles a day.

Middleton had his staff prepare a detailed operational plan for the occupation of Brittany and the defeat of the 60,000 German troops still in his path. The 6th Armored Division would push along the northern coast of Brittany to Brest, with the 83rd Infantry Division following behind. The 4th Armored and 8th Infantry Divisions would push south and then swing along Brittany's southern coast to Quiberon and Lorient. Task Force A, under Brigadier Herbert Earnest, was to make a dash to seize a key railway viaduct near the port city of St-Malo, which would then be captured before Middleton's troops headed west for Brest itself.

Caution was not what Patton had in mind. Armed with intelligence from Ultra, Patton was convinced that the

German forces in Brittany were a disorganized rabble with little armour, artillery or air support. Pockets of resistance could be quickly bypassed and mopped up later. His troops had little to fear from German counterattacks. Patton even made a five-pound wager with Montgomery that his troops could be in Brest in five days. One area that did concern Patton were reports that the Germans would try to capture and destroy key bridges and dams ahead of his spearheads, so he gave XIX Tactical Air Command the job of monitoring them and driving off any threats.

On the afternoon of 1 August Patton had caught up with the 6th Armored's commander, Robert Grow, at a roadside outside Avranches. He pulled Grow to one side and ordered him to take Brest and not worry about intermediate objectives. "Bypass resistance," said Patton, overriding Middleton's orders for Grow to first take St-Malo and the nearby town of Dinan.

■ *Above:* **Patton's drive to Brest was characterized by rapid armoured thrusts that kept the Germans off-balance.**

The war diary of Grow's 68th Tank Battalion records that, throughout the day, German fighter-bombers tried in vain to halt the division's columns as they moved south through Avranches:

"After moving out we were strafed by enemy planes, and suffered one casualty. It was our first experience with strafing planes, and we shot at them perhaps a little indiscriminately. Perhaps the trigger finger was a little itchy. At 19:30 hours, the column was strafed again, this time south of Avranches, but we suffered no casualties. Then, we closed down in bivouac shortly before midnight north of Antrain. The battalion S-2 [intelligence officer], Captain Raines, went forward to contact the [resistance fighters of the] French Forces of the Interior (FFI) for information and found that they had cleared the town of enemy, and had seized and held an important bridge there, vitally necessary for the continued advance of the combat command. Our Reconnaissance Platoon, commanded by Lieutenant Harry Linebaugh in the meanwhile had reconnoitred for additional crossings of the river to be used in the event the bridge was blown. So ended another day, and we were really starting to roll."

The charge for Brest

XIX Tactical Air Command's fighter-bombers could not get airborne until late on the afternoon of 1 August because of bad weather, but as soon as they arrived over Grow's columns they made their mark. German anti-aircraft guns hidden in hay wagons were hit, and then three deadly 88mm flak guns blocking 6th Armored's route were taken out.

After issuing brief orders to his senior officers during that night, Grow led the 6th Armored into Brittany early the following morning. He pushed his columns along side roads to bypass German troops at a breakneck speed. The 6th Armored formed into two columns, with Combat Command A on the left, and moved out for Brest. The only delays were caused by roadblocks and small minefields which were easily bypassed. Several small skirmishes broke out, but Grow's troopers easily brushed aside the disorganized and poorly armed German resistance.

The value of air support

One of Grow's combat commands made 48km (30 miles) during 2 August and another 24km (15 miles) the following day. They ran into virtually no opposition thanks to Ultra intercepts, which alerted Patton to German deployments in Brittany. Patton was stretching the rules governing the use of this highly secret intelligence in such a way, but he was determined to maximize the speed of his advance. XIX Tactical Air Command fighter-bombers also patrolled far ahead of Grow's columns, confirming that they had an open road. Patton ordered his airmen not to bomb any bridges in case this hindered Grow's advance.

The 6th Armored's rapid advance across Brittany outstripped the routine planning cycle for air support, so Otto Weyland's airmen could no longer rely on detailed briefings before they took off on their missions. They had to rely on updates on the battle situation from tactical air liaison officers with the armoured spearheads as they approached the battlefield. In this fluid situation, rapid recognition of friendly tanks was essential, so Patton's tanks were issued with large cerise and yellow panels to ease identification.

Over the next five days, Weyland's flyers provided invaluable support for Patton's columns racing through Brittany, hitting 21 German troop concentrations, 1 command post, 250 motor vehicles, 12 tanks, 4 locomotives

and 9 railway cars. These air strikes were nowhere near as intense as during later battles in France, but the timeliness of them often turned the battle in Patton's favour and prevented small German forces holding up American columns on narrow roads. The destruction of seven Tiger tanks on the morning of 2 August by P-47 Thunderbolts was typical, because it meant Patton's men did not have to spend a day hunting them down, and suffering losses, but could instead speed westwards.

The 68th Tank Battalion's war diary gives a flavour of the hell-for-leather advance of 6th Armored:

"On 3 August, we moved out at 12:25 hours, Company 'A,' marching with the advance guard, had been receiving continuous small-arms fire, but Captain Polk had found it necessary to use only limited deployment to clear the route of march. However, upon entering Mauron, one platoon, as part of the advance party, encountered stiff small-arms and cannon fire. So, with this platoon acting as a base of fire, the remainder of the company enveloped the town from the north. During this action, they destroyed several machine-gun nests and caused heavy enemy casualties. As a result of this attack, what

■ *Above:* A disabled German Panther tank in Brittany. The Panther, though a formidable tank, was still vulnerable to attacks from the rear and flank.

■ *Right:* Two concealed German grenadiers with their 7.62mm MG42 keep an eye out for US troops.

■ Above: With an M4 Sherman escort, US troops pass destroyed German armour on their way across Brittany.

was left of this Kraut force fell back from the town. And here's an interesting note – for the first time we found that quite a few of the heinies were wearing Red Cross arm bands. Was Jerry getting a little desperate – maybe? Well, when this action was completed, the battalion moved into bivouac one-and-a-half kilometers (one mile) south of Mauron at 22:00 hours. At this time, one platoon, the second, of Company 'D' was assigned to 'Combat Command A' trains for rearguard protection. Our supply lines were stretching a wee bit."

Middleton was 160km (100 miles) behind the spearheads and had not yet been fully briefed by Patton, so was not happy to hear that Grow's troops were not attacking Dinan and St-Malo as he had ordered. During the night of 2 August, he countermanded Patton's

orders to take Brest and forced Grow to halt and prepare to attack Dinan on the following day, even though his spearheads had gone well past the town. When Patton arrived at Grow's headquarters on 3 August to find his orders had been countermanded, he was far from pleased and again ordered the 6th Armored to head for Brest.

For a day Grow's division halted while Middleton issued orders and counter-orders over a very unreliable radio link. A whole 24 hours was lost before the 6th Armored started out for Brest again.

The 68th Tank Battalion's historians take up the story. "At nine-thirty on the 5th of August, Combat Command A resumed its westward trek under the command of Brigadier-General James Taylor. Then east of Merdrignac,

■ *Left:* American soldiers conduct urban operations within the city of St-Malo. The greatest hazards to US troops in urban environments were booby-traps and German snipers.

■ *Below:* A damaged US M5 tank is towed onto an M19 tractor. Armoured vehicles required a great deal of repair and maintenance.

Company 'C' was fired on by organized sniper fire from a trench system. The company immediately returned fire, killing five enemy, and wounded many others. When the head of the column reached Huelgoat, Lieutenant-Colonel McCorrison was ordered by the Division Commander to clear the town, and two platoons of Company 'A' were ordered to support one company of the 44th in accomplishing this mission. This force closed on the enemy in two directions and drove them into the northern end of the town. At this point, resistance grew very stiff, and the task force came to grips with the enemy at close quarters. One tank was hit by Panzerfaust fire at a very close range, and was set on fire. However, the tank crew remained inside and continued to machine-gun the Krauts until the heat became unbearable; crawling out of the vehicle they found themselves surrounded by Wehrmacht troops who

called to them to surrender. Unanimously they refused, and immediately opened fire on the group in the face of overwhelming odds, and almost certain death. Technician 5th Grade, Santo De Nunziato and Fred K. Blaylock were cut down by machine-gun fire. Nunziato was immediately killed and Blaylock died of wounds later in the hospital. Technician 4th Grade Charles E. Pidcock continued to fire his submachine gun at close range until his tank exploded, and threw him into a nearby hedgerow. The enemy had been dissipated; all three tankers were later awarded the Silver Star for their gallantry in action.

"After the above action the column passed through the town of Huelgoat and bypassed the fighting, Company C commanded by Captain Daniel E. Smith was ordered to relieve Company A as part of the advance Guard. The actual transfer, however, did not take

■ *Above:* **The Third Army's thrust across northern France resulted in the capture of thousands of German prisoners. This was an enormous logistical headache for the Allied commanders.**

90

■ *Right:* American soldiers hoist the US flag over the town of St-Malo after the 800-strong German garrison surrendered following a two-week siege.

place until next morning, and that night enemy patrols infiltrated through a company bivouac area in the forward area, throwing grenades and causing one casualty before being driven off."

Ultra information came in on 4 August reporting the Germans in full retreat along the northern coast of Brittany heading towards Brest, so Patton immediately dispatched Task Force A to pursue them to the gates of the objective. Reports from the French resistance and Ultra on the following day reported the presence of a regiment of 2000 élite German paratroopers at Carhaix, on Grow's route, so Patton ordered him to dodge past them using the many sideroads.

By late on 6 August Grow's spearheads were on the outskirts of Brest, and began probing its outer defences. Grow ordered Combat Command B to put in an attack at first light in the hope of bouncing the

defenders into surrendering. The Germans, though, were waiting and sent the attacks reeling back. After a day being shelled by German artillery, Grow was convinced that a major attack was needed but it would take two days to mass his forces. In the meantime, Grow sent forward an emissary under a white flag to demand the surrender of the garrison. The German garrison commander politely declined his offer.

Outside Brest, the 68th Tank Battalion was poised for action. "Early on the morning of 8 August, the advance guard, to which was attached Company 'C' and one platoon of Company 'D', was heavily shelled by enemy artillery, direct fire and heavy mortar fire," recorded its historians. "Our vehicles were immobilized because of lack of gasoline; our drive had gone so far and so fast·that our supply lines were stretched almost to breaking point. Jerry had excellent observation, and his

Left: General Patton allowed his corps commanders to devise their own plans of attack, merely informing them of their objectives. Though he allowed tactical freedom, he made sure his commanders drove forward relentlessly.

gun batteries were perfectly camouflaged; his ground troops were well dug-in. And, although liaison planes vainly attempted to spot the concealed positions, our counter-battery fire was ineffective, and the merciless pounding continued for four-and-a-half hours without respite. During this action many acts of heroism were noted; for example: Captain Daniel E. Smith, Company Commander of Company 'C', attempted to locate enemy installations, boldly stood on tank and hedgerow, and so exposed himself on countless occasions without concern for his personal safety.

"Attack and seize Brest"

"An infantry attack was expected; we needed better observation. Sensing this Captain Smith maintained constant watch, paying no heed to the hail of shells bursting about him. For this heroic conduct, he was later awarded the Silver Star Medal. Also, Private First Class James T. Smith discovered that his buddy lay wounded in a slit trench; he climbed on top of the turret of his tank to find the first aid kit. A shell struck the turret and seriously wounded him. Despite his mortal wounds, he secured the kit and crawled to the aid of his fallen comrade. Then, after treating his buddy, he collapsed and was himself evacuated. Several days later, he died in a field hospital. For his gallantry in action, he was posthumously awarded the Silver Star Medal.

"During this costly action, our reconnaissance had further ascertained that we had run into outer defences of fortress Brest. The Division objective loomed so near and yet so far. Our commanders followed the only logical course – withdrawal to more advantageous positions, stabilize our line, and prepare to attack this strategically important port. It should be noted here that the final reduction of Brest later proved to be a major military operation requiring the commitment of a reinforced corps and lasting several weeks. And here we were – having nearly completed a [400-kilometer] 250-mile 'pile driving' breakthrough which had sapped our armored virility. The men were tired. Then from higher headquarters came the order to our Battalion to 'attack and seize that portion of Brest which lies within your zone'. Automatically plans were made and we prepared for what we thought would be a last, futiley suicidal, sacrificial dash to glory."

Securing the supply lines

As Grow was organizing his troops for the attack, bypassed German troops began attacking his supply lines. Then a patrol managed to capture a German staff car complete with the commander of the 266th Infantry Division and his key staff. They had been conducting a reconnaissance for a move into Brest from their base on Brittany's northern coast. The 6th Armored turned around and launched a violent attack against the now leaderless German force, breaking it up and capturing thousands of prisoners.

Combat Command B led the attack, which was preceded by a heavy artillery preparation, early on the morning of 9 August. German 20mm flak guns held up the first wave of the American assault until they were silenced by US artillery fire. In the confused fighting, a German unit surprised a US column from the 44th and 9th Armored Infantry Battalions. The 68th Tank Battalion now arrived on the scene to lead a counterattack, sending companies to outflank the German stronghold of Plouvien. Soon the American tank crews and armoured infantrymen were locked in close-quarter combat that lasted most of the day. Eventually the 6th Armored's superior firepower and *élan* won the day and drove out the Germans. Fighter-bombers of XIX Tactical Air Command now swooped on the retreating Germans to work them over, thus ending any enemy hopes of breaking the US grip on Brest.

The 6th Armored's victory

Events elsewhere now overtook Grow's plans to seize Brest and he was ordered to contain the German garrison, while moving the rest of his force to secure Lorient and the southern coast of Brittany. Patton's daring thrust to Brest had failed and Montgomery was five pounds better off. The 6th Armored, however, had totally unhinged the German defences in Brittany and prevented the peninsula serving as a rear base to attack the Allies in France. For the loss of only 130 killed and 400 wounded it had taken more than 4000 prisoners. Patton was now getting into his stride and feeling a lot more confident, commenting to an aide after inspecting war debris on 7 August 1944: "Just look at that. Could anything be more magnificent? God, how I love it."

Middleton had to make do with using Earnest's task force of cavalry scouts and tank destroyers to first seal St-Malo until the 83rd Division could arrive in strength and complete its capture. According to the official history of the 83rd Division's 331st Infantry Regiment, "12,000 Germans defended the walled city, and they vowed to 'fight to the last stone'". It would take two weeks of street fighting to raze St-Malo, involving all of the 83rd Division supported by parts of Task Force A, and elements of the 8th Infantry Division. XIX Tactical Air Command's fighter-bombers were called in to support these attacks, sinking two German warships and striking the numerous concrete bunkers surrounding the port. On 6 August, the Germans demolished all the quays, locks, breakwaters and harbour machinery and set fire to the city. On 9

August, the enemy defenders were forced back to the Citadel at St-Servan and to Dinard on the west bank of the river just opposite St-Malo. There they held the GIs at bay from underground pillboxes and camouflaged strongpoints. Days of house-to-house fighting under thick smoke, artillery fire and fighter-bomber attacks could not convince the Germans to give up. Finally, direct hits by 8in guns destroyed much of the enemy artillery and machine-gun emplacements and forced them to surrender. Frank Reichmann in the 1st Battalion of the 331st recorded that "a platoon of captured Germans started singing farewell to their commander. Most of them were in tears."

Three divisions, the 2nd, 8th and 29th Infantry, took until 25 August to capture Brest along with 38,000 Germans. In the process the vital port and much of the city were destroyed.

The advance by John Wood's 4th Armored Division towards Rennes was equally as dramatic as Grow's race to Brest. Again Ultra information was the key to Patton's strategy after it reported that the Germans were to "begin at once" destroying their supply dumps at Rennes. Wood was told to pull out all the stops to get there as fast as possible.

Wood's troopers were moving so fast they exceeded their assigned movement rate and almost led to their being mistaken for a German column. Patton tasked his air commander, Weyland, with sending three fighter-bomber groups to take them out, but fortunately the lead pilots recognized Wood's Shermans and waved off their attack. They then swooped ahead of the column knocking out several German roadblocks backed by 88mm flak guns.

By 2 August Wood's men had arrived at Rennes to find it heavily defended by a strong German garrison. Rein-forcements would be needed to dislodge them, so Wood began looking for a way around the city. The lack of resistance

■ *Below:* **US tanks and infantry search a French village ahead for German positions.**

■ *Above:* A German officer inspects the damage to a US Sherman tank. German tank fire was so effective against the M4, that the Sherman crews nicknamed their machines "Ronsons", after the lighter, due to their habit of catching fire when hit.

elsewhere in southern Brittany made him and Middleton think that it was perhaps a waste of an armoured division to use Wood's outfit to mop up this objective. The two commanders began to position the 4th Armored to push eastwards, when Patton intervened and ordered the advance to Lorient. The Third Army commander still did not feel confident enough to openly challenge Bradley's orders to use all of VIII Corps to deal with Brittany. Wood was furious, complaining that his division was attacking the wrong way.

On 3 August, 2000 Germans pulled out of Rennes after setting fire to their supply dumps and retreated into Brittany. Wood's troopers were hard on their heels. XIX Tactical Air Command

dealt with a counterattack by 15 German tanks on 4 August and Wood's men rolled on. The following day they were in Vannes on the Bay of Biscay, cutting the last escape route of Hitler's Brittany garrison. Wood then pushed on later in the day to Lorient, to be rebuffed by the German defenders.

Corporal Albert O. Maranda of the 4th Armored Division's 94th Armored Field Artillery Battalion recorded the heady days of the advance to the Atlantic coast in his diary.

"*2 August:* Managed to get six hours' sleep. Finally got shaved and washed. Only intermittent artillery fire, no response from Jerry artillery. 21 German planes came over. We managed to keep them away from our area with machine-gun fire. It's the first time I have been able to fire on one of their planes. We are moving slowly into Rennes. Moved a couple miles back from our present location – Jerries have us spotted. After getting dug in, guns in position, etc., it was midnight before I got to bed. Took about 200 prisoners. Mail finally caught up, letter from Ma.

3 August: Was alerted, expected to pull out – might bypass Rennes and go on to St-Nazaire or Vannes. Didn't pull out. Shelled a position where 500 Jerries were located. They were called upon to surrender but they didn't. A few French Moroccan soldiers attached to us. They had been prisoners of the Nazis. Laid around and slept – need it bad. Rained most of day, cleared at night. Nazi planes came over but didn't bother us.

4 August: Laid around expecting to pull out. A lot of attached outfits catching up to us. 155mm, anti-aircraft & 240mm guns. Caught up on all the small-arms maintenance. More mail came in, also newspapers. Letter from Ma, Francis & Shirley. The papers aren't allowed to mention this outfit as we are in the spearhead position. Rennes captured, first column of the Division are right after them. 2000 prisoners taken.

5 August: Expect to pull out for sure today and head for Vannes – a [120-kilometer] 75-mile run. First column is just outside the city. Pulled out at 15:07 hours, went down to La Gacilly where we bivouacked for the night. A B-Battery self-propelled gun fell out with a broken drive shaft so we left it. Towed another one in with minor ailments. Got to bed at 24:30 hours. Weather has been very nice.

■ *Right:* A French Resistance member (far left) offers advice to US infantry and a tank crew concerning the whereabouts of enemy armour.

■ *Left:* US infantry move forward beside their tanks through a cloud of smoke and dust on a road near Coutances during the Allied drive to the Brest peninsula.

■ *Below:* A US trooper walks beside an accompanying tank. Soldiers liked to ride aboard their supporting armour, though this behaviour was not officially endorsed.

6 August: Weather swell. Pulled out of bivouac at 06:15 hours, through Rockefort [sic.], down to three miles outside Vannes. Free French helped our boys to capture the city. Some have German rifles, others had guns dropped to them by the British to help us get the stragglers. Went swimming at the beach just outside the city, sure felt good."

Meanwhile, Wood was given permission by Middleton to probe eastwards to the outskirts of Nantes on the River Loire, so long as he kept his troops out of the city. Colonel Bruce Clarke's Combat Command A raced 130km (80 miles) to the city only to find the Germans were in the process of blowing up their supply dumps and bases. After French Resistance fighters alerted Clarke to a safe route though German lines, Wood gave Clarke permission to try to storm the city. In a matter of hours the 4th Armored was in control of the city and the gateway to the Loire valley.

It would be another week before Wood and his men were finally relieved of responsibility for standing guard outside Lorient and St-Nazaire by the US 6th Armored Division, which in turn was replaced by the 3rd Infantry Division in late August. The two outposts and 27,000 Germans would remain besieged by US and French troops until the German surrender in May 1945. In the course of two weeks, Wood's men captured 5000 Germans and destroyed or captured 250 enemy vehicles. The division lost only 98 dead and 362 wounded.

The drive east

As VIII Corps surged into Brittany, Patton began manoeuvring Haislip's XV Corps through Avranches to connect the Third Army's left flank with Courtney Hodges' First Army, which was pushing due east towards Mortain. The mission of Haislip's corps kept evolving on a day-by-day basis as Patton's ambitions developed.

In the days after the capture of Avranches, the 90th Infantry had swung through the town and taken up blocking positions to the east to protect the key road centre. The slow progress of First Army units pushing eastwards mean that Avranches was the only road south for Patton's troops. In spite of efforts by military police and senior Third Army officers to bring order to the traffic chaos in Avranches, it was still proving very slow to move units through the town.

The Seine beckons

As traffic congestion eased, the 79th Infantry Division had moved into line to the south of the 90th Division, to be followed by the 5th Armored Division. The positioning of this strong strike force south of Avranches and facing eastwards would soon offer Patton a chance to put his ideas for a drive to the Seine into action. Ultra reported that Laval and Le Mans were not yet being prepared for defence, and no German combat units were blocking any Third Army drive eastwards to the Seine. Patton did not want to let this opportunity slip out of his grasp.

Eisenhower, Montgomery and Bradley were all now beginning to see the opportunities offered by unleashing Patton's armour in a race to the Seine. Over 2 and 3 August Eisenhower and Montgomery agreed that there was now a real possibility of rolling up the eastern flank of the German forces in Normandy. Bradley concurred, and the following day he issued new orders to Patton. XV Corps was now to drive southeast through Mayenne and Laval with Le Mans as its ultimate objective. Once XV Corps had cleared its current position, there would be room for Walton Walker's XX Corps to move through Avranches and push south to

Nantes and Angers to protect both Haislip and Middleton from counter-attack by German armour south of the Loire River.

Patton briefed Haislip on his new mission on 3 August, and warned him that he might receive new orders at any time to swing north or northeast to trap German troops south of Caen. Patton clearly had his eyes set on destroying the Germans in a battle of encirclement west of the Seine. Montgomery was also beginning to think the same way, but Bradley was more cautious about pushing Patton's troops out on a limb in any pincer move. In the meantime, Patton told XV Corps it was to keep going and not stop for anything. Radio messages to the French Resistance alerted them to be ready to help Patton's tanks as they raced for Le Mans.

As the Allies were recasting their plans, the Germans were also beginning to realize the danger posed by Patton's move through Avranches. The drive on Le Mans threatened the main supply base of the German Seventh Army and, if left unchecked, Patton's tanks could either press on to Paris or turn north to surround the Fifth Panzer Army fighting around Caen.

Many senior German officers in Normandy, including Günther von Kluge and Paul Hausser, now saw that the game was up and a retreat should be ordered to allow a new defensive line to be set up. True to form, Hitler would not countenance any idea of a retreat. He ordered a counterattack to be launched to cut the narrow lifeline to Patton's troops at Avranches. Five armoured divisions, including at least two élite Waffen-SS units, with some 185 tanks were to be pulled out of the line opposite the British and sent westwards to strike at the Americans around Mortain. Advancing from southern France towards the Loire were

■ *Above:* Troops of the US Third Army move though the ruins of Le Mans. Behind them German storerooms are still smouldering hours after the action.

■ *Right:* Grateful French citizens of Le Mans rush out into the street to greet US troops. This strange experience could be both exciting and unnerving for the young American GIs.

100

the 9th Panzer and 708th Infantry Divisions, who were given the mission of containing and destroying Patton's armoured spearheads.

Kluge thought the Avranches counterattack was madness. His panzer divisions were shattered after more than six weeks of non-stop action with no relief. Most had fewer than 25 percent of their tanks ready for battle, petrol and ammunition were in short supply and Allied air supremacy would make it impossible to concentrate the attack force in secret. Once alerted to the threat, Kluge thought Allied fighter-bombers would devastate his panzer columns. Hitler, however, was adamant. Operation Luttich, as the attack was codenamed, would go ahead regardless of the complaints of the commanders on the ground in Normandy. The Führer's orders must be carried out. In the climate of fear in the Wehrmacht after the 20 July Bomb Plot, no one wanted to be seen to be refusing a "Führer order". Hausser was given overall command of the attack, which was to begin on 6 August.

XV Corps strikes

When it began to move forward on 5 August, all that lay in XV Corps' path were scattered German logistic support units at Mayenne and Laval, as well as Luftwaffe flak batteries. Hausser sent a senior officer to Le Mans to organize the defence of the Seventh Army's rear logistic headquarters, but he only just arrived as Patton's tanks were about to enter the town.

Haislip opened his attack before the 5th Armored was fully ready because he was determined to get to Le Mans before the German reinforcements, including the 11th Panzer Division, arrived from the south of France.

XIX Tactical Air Command used Ultra intelligence to strike at targets in the path of XV Corps, putting a major effort into knocking out the large German airfields at Le Mans and Angers, which were being used by Luftwaffe ground-attack squadrons. These were the only heavy German firepower standing in Patton's way and he wanted them put out of action. Weyland's reconnaissance planes ranged far ahead of Haislip's columns, trying to confirm information from Ultra and, if necessary, neutralizing any threats to Patton's thinly spread and exposed forces.

Maintaining air cover

The tempo of operations reached a new height during this period, with Weyland's command flying in excess of 600 sorties a day and some pilots pulling a 12-hour duty in the cockpits of their P-47s and P-51s. Weyland reported "good hunting, especially in tanks" during the XV Corps advance on Le Mans. A new élite squadron of Mustangs, modified to fire rockets, joined Weyland to increased his air-borne strike forces, and P-61 Black Widow night-fighters were also drafted in to protect the Avranches "choke-point" bridges from nocturnal raids by German bombers. As the Third Army advanced deeper into France, Weyland had to start moving his airstrips forward to keep his planes in range of Patton's armoured spearheads.

The job of taking Mayenne was given to Raymond McLain's 90th Infantry Division. He had taken command of the division only a few days earlier after Patton had relieved his predecessor. The outfit had taken heavy casualties in the Bocage battles and was treated warily by Patton's staff. McLain proved his mettle during the next few days, though. He pushed his division forward with great enthusiasm and they rose to the occasion. Their truck convoys darted across the French countryside, bypassing German road-blocks and in less than half a day had

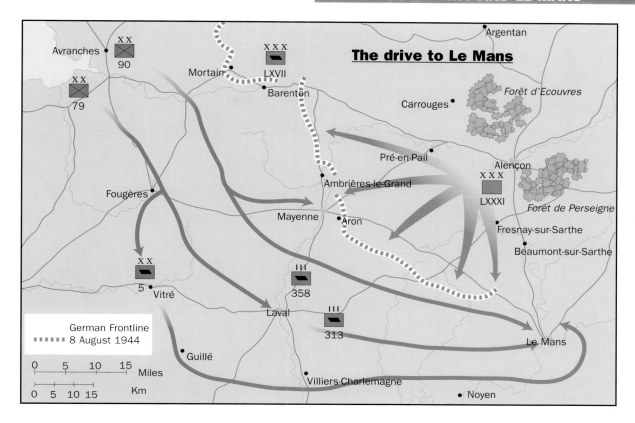

The drive to Le Mans

German Frontline
••••••• 8 August 1944

0   5   10   15   Miles
0   5   10 15   Km

■ *Above:* **The drive to Le Mans epitomized Patton's armoured warfare tactics.**

travelled 48km (30 miles) to enter the town of Mayenne.

To the south, Ira Wyche's 79th Division also raced forward in truck columns, reaching Laval to find the Germans had already left. They soon linked up with the French Resistance and found a dam intact across the River Mayenne. Within hours Haislip's engineers had floated a bridge across the river to open the way to Le Mans. Next day the advance continued at the same breakneck pace, with Haislip ordering his officers "to push all personnel to the limit of human endurance".

Leading the 5th Armored Division was the 81st Tank Battalion, part of an armour-infantry task force, led by its commanding officer Lieutenant-Colonel Leroy Anderson. The unit's war diary recorded the chaotic scenes as it approached Le Mans:

"Task Force Anderson advanced through the day without meeting any hostile troops, until late in the

afternoon. Just as Lieutenant Leonard Keene, who was at the point for 'B' Company, approached a bridge across the River Mayenne, south of Laval, he saw two German cars driving along the road just ahead of him. His tank immediately opened fire and knocked out the cars. Close examination a little later showed that the vehicles were loaded with demolition charges to be used in blowing up the bridge that had just been crossed.

"In a short time a group of French civilians gathered and were given the rifles, food and clothing that were found in the German cars. This soon became accepted policy in France. Most of the civilians were only too glad to join the French Forces of the Interior (FFI) in hunting down scattered German soldiers and turning them over to the liberating forces. Similarly, they hadn't had any new shoes or clothing for several years, and were happy to get the Wehrmacht equipment.

■ Above: US troops transfer fuel from a railroad tanker to five-gallon jerrycans. These jerrycans were then taken to the Third Army's advancing armoured forces.

"The great tank-infantry team made an impressive sight to the citizens of the newly liberated towns. To show their appreciation, the civilians threw flowers to all of the vehicles and at every short halt gave cider, wine, cognac, and even champagne to their liberators. Large Tricolor flags were taken from hiding and flown from windows and roof tops. Signs were erected saying 'Welcome to our Liberators' and *'Vive la France, Vive L'Amérique'*. It was a happy day for the civilians as the Americans came by. Frequently one village would telephone ahead to the next and when the

Battalion entered the next town flags would be flying and people would throng the streets. Many times it was more like a parade than a fight."

The advance guard of German reinforcements now tried to intercept XV Corps and protect Le Mans. The reconnaissance battalion of the 9th Panzer and a marching regiment of the 708th Infantry went into action against the two spearhead battalions of the 90th Infantry Division. In a brief but violent battle the American forces outflanked the Germans and trapped them in a wood. By the time the battle was over some 1200 Germans emerged waving white flags. While this battle was at its height, the 79th Division's trucks had reached the outskirts of Le Mans.

To speed up the advance of the 79th and 90th Divisions, Haislip had drafted in more than 100 trucks from the 5th Armored's motor pool. Vital fuel and other supplies were dumped to make room for the GIs on the trucks, playing havoc with the division's logistics. This delayed the 5th Armored's refuelling east of Laval and meant it might not be ready to support the attack on Le Mans. Eventually, 100,000 gallons of fuel had been delivered to Lundford Oliver's division. With its fuel tanks full, the division raced ahead and, by 8 August, was up with the rest of XV Corps for the attack on Le Mans the following morning. A brief skirmish with a couple of German tanks outside Laval did not delay the division's advance, but a lack of military maps meant Oliver's men had to use Michelin tourist guides to direct their race to Le Mans.

The XV Corps attack saw the 79th and 90th Divisions move into Le Mans from the west, while the 5th Armored pushed tank columns to the north and south of the city to cut off any German retreat. After commandeering local river craft, the first GIs entered the city's western suburbs, only to find the place largely deserted of Germans and 75,000 grateful citizens starting to fill the streets to welcome them. The 5th Armored then closed the ring around the city and protected its eastern approaches, engaging German tanks and knocking out six of them.

"For three hours CCA went by"

When the 5th Armored reached Le Mans, the 81st Tank Battalion was part of the assault force. Its war diary recounts the attack:

"At Arnage, Combat Command A (CCA) crossed in front of the column from Combat Command B's (CCB's) right flank to the left flank, in order to cut off the approaches to Le Mans from the west and north. For three hours CCA went by. When the road was clear again, Lieutenant-Colonel Anderson left his command post at Arnage and ordered 'C' Company into Le Mans, while 'B' company blocked the roads to

■ *Right:* Huge convoys of trucks were needed to transport vital fuel supplies to Patton's tanks. Here, a US truck leads 40 others loaded with fuel to the frontline.

the southeast. 'A' Company, which had followed Task Force Anderson, passed through 'B' and 'C' Companies and established roadblocks east of the city on highway N-157. At 18:00 hours Lieutenant Howard Miller led his platoon of 'C' Company tankers up N-23 into the city.

"At the Gnome-Rhone aircraft factory and airfield located at the southern edge of this important rail terminal city, a few Germans tried to hold off the column, but Lieutenant Paul Dreisbach's mortar men knew how to deal with them. Huge bomb craters provided covered firing positions for the enemy. Infantry would not have a chance if it tried to dig out the Germans, and the big craters made it too difficult to try to use the tanks. This was the time to use the mortars from Headquarters Company. A heavy barrage was laid down using a mixture

of white phosphorus and heavy high-explosive ammo. When the Germans tried to run the tankers machine gunned them and the infantry picked them off with their rifles.

"Thirty minutes after the fight started the column was on the move again. By 20:00 hours the city had been liberated. The 79th Infantry Division mopped up the city, but the southern suburbs yielded about 200 prisoners of war to 'C' Company. By midnight Service Company had evacuated the prisoners to the rear. All of the roadblocks were well established. At noon the following day, after a quiet but very dark night, the task forces assembled east of the city and prepared to continue the drive to Paris."

In the space of three days Haislip's men had advanced more than 120km (75 miles) and taken the strategic town of Le Mans for little loss. Several

■ *Above:* German artillery in action during the Brittany campaign. Despite the camouflage, German batteries were very vulnerable to US fighter-bombers.

thousand German troops had also been captured. Patton was now poised to strike either eastwards to the Seine or turn north towards Caen to trap the German forces in Normandy.

XV Corps' advance had opened the way for Walker's XX Corps to push south to the banks of the Loire at Angers. The 5th Infantry Division was ordered to send a regimental combat team to seize the town on 7 August after Ultra reported that the Germans were pulling out and the road south was wide open.

A new German threat

By 6 August Hausser's battered panzer divisions had managed to break free from their previous positions south of Caen and began moving eastwards. Fuel shortages and air attacks meant only three of the assault divisions were in place on time. The desperate situation around Le Mans meant Hausser had little choice but to strike before he was ready on the following morning.

Hitler had originally dispatched the orders for Operation Luttich by courier to Kluge's headquarters, so Ultra did not pick up any indication of the impending offensive until the attacking divisions started issuing orders to their sub-units on the evening of 6 August.

Patton, along with other Allied commanders, only began to learn of the impending German attack later that night when the first Ultra intercepts started to filter through to the special intelligence detachment in his headquarters. The Third Army's special intelligence officer, Major Melvin Helfers, and his boss, Colonel Oscar Koch, rushed into their general's quarters with the latest reports on the planned German attack against the First Army at Mortain. This was the first time Helfers had briefed Patton and, in future, the general would draw even more heavily on this source of intelligence. Helfers commented that he was the only Ultra officer "in all the US armies who daily briefed the Third Army commander directly".

Realizing that his army's lifeline was being threatened if the First Army division at Mortain could not hold its line, Patton immediately called up the commander of his XX Corps, Walker, whose three divisions were at that moment moving down towards Avranches, driving behind the threatened sector. Walker was ordered to deploy his divisions, the 35th and 80th Infantry Divisions, as well as the 2nd Free French Armoured Division, to act as a backstop for the First Army. Patton also alerted his air commander, Otto, to be prepared to switch all his aircraft to deal with the German threat. By midnight, XIX Tactical Air Command pilots were being briefed on their targets for the following morning.

The German attack

Well before first light the first German panzer spearheads had penetrated American lines (at 01:00 hours on 7 August the lead elements of the 2nd SS Panzer Division made contact with US troops; the 1st SS Panzer *Leibstandarte*, 116th Panzer, and 17th SS Panzer-grenadier divisions also participated) and put the 30th Infantry Division under severe pressure, eventually surrounding one US battalion. After fog lifted later in the morning, Weyland's pilots and their counterparts from IX Tactical Air Command and the Royal Air Force (RAF) were in action over Mortain. Caught in broad daylight in the open, Hausser's tanks were sitting ducks and were slaughtered. The two divisions trying to reinforce the attack were particularly heavily hit and stopped in their tracks. More than 50 tanks and 100 other vehicles were destroyed by air attack, and the whole coherence of the German attack was broken. The Allied

air commanders later claimed this was the first time a ground assault had been stopped solely by airpower.

In the early afternoon, Hausser realized his attack had stalled and requested permission to pull back. Hitler was having none of this and ordered the attack to be pressed home again on 8 August. Fog kept the Allied fighters at bay for most of the morning; this allowed the Waffen-SS *Leibstandarte* Panzer Division to gain some ground. Now Hitler ordered the two divisions of II SS Panzer Corps to be pulled out of the line southwest of Caen to reinforce Operation Luttich. They also received a thorough going-over from Allied fighter-bombers, and never made it to the Mortain battlefield before Hitler finally relented and called off the offensive on 11 August.

The 35th Division, detached from Third Army, eventually spearheaded the American counterattack that broke through to the trapped US troops and drove off the remnants of Hausser's shattered army.

The trap is set

As the fighting around Mortain was nearing its climax, the Allied high command was beginning to realize that Hitler might be playing right into their hands by launching seven of his panzer divisions westwards. With Patton's tanks at Le Mans, some 96km (60 miles) to the east, a giant "pocket" of 400,000 German troops had been encircled around the Norman town of Falaise. It was now time to close the noose around the neck of Kluge's defeated and exposed army and end the fighting in northern France with the total annihilation of Hitler's forces.

CHAPTER 5

CLOSING THE FALAISE GAP

"This is better and much bigger than Sicily and so far all has gone better than I had a right to expect. L'audace, l'audace, toujours l'audace…"

Patton, 13 August 1944

The day after the German attack at Mortain, Eisenhower drove from his newly established headquarters in Normandy to visit Bradley and review strategy to complete the defeat of Hitler's forces in France.

Bradley was starting to receive reports that thousands of German troops were pulling back from Mortain, and feared that this was a prelude to a general Wehrmacht withdrawal from Normandy. At this stage he was distrustful of Ultra intelligence and was not convinced that Hitler would be so stupid as to continue to push his best panzers into action at Mortain and risk their encirclement and annihilation. He proposed to Eisenhower that Patton's XV Corps be swung north from its current eastward axis of advance to link up with the British and Canadians at Argentan, south of Falaise, to trap the two German armies in Normandy. Bradley declared this was "an opportunity that comes to a commander not more than once in a century. We're about to destroy an entire hostile army. We'll go all the way from here to the German border."

■ *Left:* Smashed German armour litters the countryside around the town of Falaise. The closing of the Falaise Gap was one of the most devastating episodes for the German Army in France, and signalled the beginning of the end of their occupation.

As he was concurring with Eisenhower, Bradley telephoned Montgomery and recommended that Patton be given new orders. Although the British general was nominally the overall Allied ground commander in Normandy, coalition politics dictated that he could not really overrule the two senior US commanders in Europe, Eisenhower and Bradley, over the employment of American troops. Despite his initial preference for a "wide envelopment" along the River Seine, Montgomery agreed to Bradley's proposal and set in train the necessary changes to his battle plans.

Patton was ordered to swing north from Le Mans on 8 August, Bradley overruling protests from the Third Army commander, who still thought a "wide encirclement" along the Seine would be a better way to trap the Germans. After Patton returned to his headquarters from a visit to the fighting in Brittany, he penned Haislip's new orders which were to be executed on 10 August. When Bradley visited Patton to explain the new orders, the disgruntled Third Army commander told his superior that a great opportunity was being missed. Nonetheless, the new orders stood.

Around Le Mans XV Corps' soldiers were, meanwhile, resting and preparing for whatever Patton had in store for them. One 5th Armored Division veteran recalled heating ration tins on the motors of vehicles or at the end of the exhaust pipe. "When time was short a K ration was broken open and eaten cold," he said. "Sometimes fresh eggs and potatoes were obtained from the French civilians by trading candy, soap

■ *Below:* US troops enter the town of Argentan, south of Falaise. The sign, riddled with bullet holes, is testament to the ferocity of the fighting.

■ *Right:* XV Corps
made good
progress against a
weakened enemy
south of Argentan.

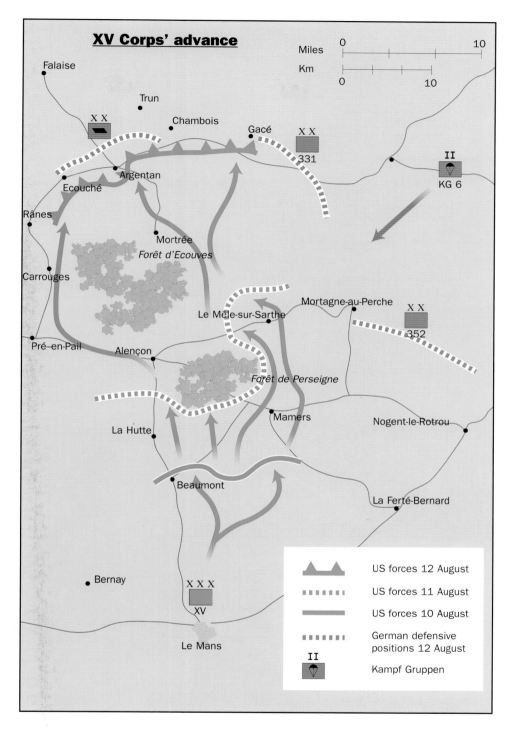

XV Corps' advance

Falaise

Trun

Chambois

Gacé

X X
331

II
KG 6

Argentan

Ecouché

Rânes

Mortrée

Forêt d'Ecouves

Carrouges

Le Mêle-sur-Sarthe

Mortagne-au-Perche

X X
352

Pré–en-Pail

Alençon

Forêt de Perseigne

La Hutte

Mamers

Nogent-le-Rotrou

Beaumont

La Ferté-Bernard

Bernay

X X X
XV

Le Mans

▲▲▲	US forces 12 August
▪▪▪▪▪	US forces 11 August
▬▬▬	US forces 10 August
▪▪▪▪▪	German defensive positions 12 August
II ⊞	Kampf Gruppen

Miles 0 — 10

Km 0 — 10

■ *Right:* XV Corps made good progress against a weakened enemy south of Argentan.

and gum. And in the apple orchards, which were frequently used as bivouac areas, swarms of yellow jackets [wasps] had to be shooed away from the food. The steel helmets with their liners removed were used as wash basins. Men slept in their clothes; they stretched out on their bedding rolls, spread on the ground, with their small arms always within reach."

To see his men on their way, Patton drove to Le Mans to brief Haislip on the

attack, which he termed "historic". The 2nd Free French Armoured Division was switched to XV Corps from XX Corps for the operation, and was to lead the left axis of the advance with Carrouges as its objective. The US 90th Division, in turn, would move up on the left flank of the French tank force. On the right, the 5th Armored Division was to aim for Alençon and ultimately Sées, with the 79th Infantry Division close behind.

In the path of Haislip's men were the battered divisions of the German LXXXI Corps defending Alençon, including the remnants of the 708th Infantry, Panzer Lehr and 9th Panzer divisions. They were positioned to the southwest of Alençon trying to hold a line linking up with Hausser's Seventh Army to the east of Mortain, and to cover German logistic units escaping northwards from Le Mans.

The advance from Le Mans

Orders were issued to XV Corps' troops during 9 August, and it took several hours for information to filter down to frontline units. The commanding officer of the 5th Armored's 81st Tank Battalion, Lieutenant-Colonel Leroy Anderson, gathered his staff and company commanders in the blacked-out dining room of a French house during the evening and issued his orders. By midnight everything was set and the battalion moved out. Progress was slow, though, as the column moved to its start points.

On 10 August, XV Corps was ready to go, and the attack commenced at 08:00 hours. The corps began a relentless advance north from Le Mans. There was no organized resistance, only

■ Left: US troops scramble through the ruins of a destroyed house as they engage enemy forces. Urban warfare was a slow and painstaking process.

a series of disjointed skirmishes with small groups of German defenders and fleeing truck convoys. US fighter-bombers roamed ahead of Patton's tank columns, strafing retreating German columns. While this added to the panic in the ranks of the Germans, the wreckage considerably hindered XV Corps' advance.

Futile German resistance

The 5th Armored crossed the line of departure on time with Combat Command A on the left and Combat Command Reserve on the right, and at 11:00 hours both columns were meeting strong armoured and artillery resistance from 9th Panzer. Some 50 enemy tanks were active, and several counterattacks were repulsed in securing river crossings. German anti-tank guns were positioned at road junctions to try to hold up the American advance, but to little avail. Nine German tanks and two armoured cars were destroyed, 84 enemy troops were killed and 116 captured.

According to the 81st Tank Battalion's history, it caught up with the tail-end of the German 5th Artillery Training Battalion just before noon.

"This artillery battalion had horse-drawn artillery pieces and was caught on the move. Just as Lieutenant Miller spotted the tail of the column, a concealed 88mm anti-tank gun opened up on him, and the first round hit the turret of his tank. The blast of the high-explosive shell knocked Captain Guthrie off the tank and killed Lieutenant Martin, the infantry platoon leader, who was also on the rear deck of the tank. A few quick rounds from Corporal Louis Cannata's tank gun quieted the German gun. Lieutenant Miller's third platoon then moved out and overran the German column, killing fifty men of the Wehrmacht, and destroying nine horses, seven 105mm howitzers, two caissons, one motorcycle

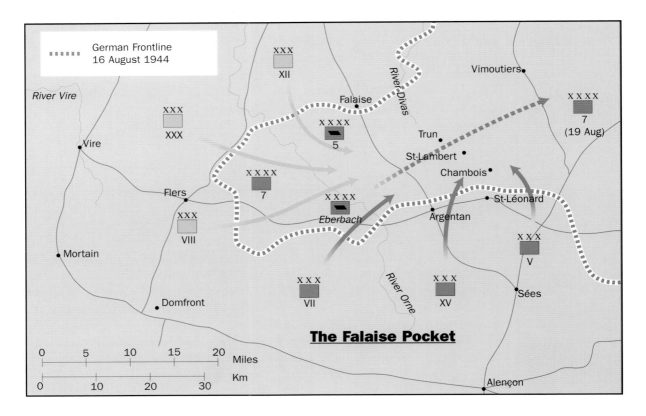

The Falaise Pocket

German Frontline 16 August 1944

■ **Above: The movement of German and Allied forces during the closing of the Falaise Pocket.**

half-track, and one truck. Lieutenant Victor Anderson led his first platoon around to the right of the third platoon, and caught the remainder of the German artillery battalion on another road. First his platoon hit the front of the column, then the rear, and then the middle. After that it was just a matter of time before every bit of German equipment was smashed."

German troops were steadily withdrawing during the day and kept moving into the evening, with spearheads of the 5th Armored and 79th Infantry close on their heels. When the German rearguards turned to fight they inflicted losses on their pursuers. Senior US officers were forward with their assault troops encouraging them to keep on advancing. This resulted in a battalion commander and a battalion executive officer from the 5th Armored being seriously wounded.

The 81st Tank Battalion's Lieutenant-Colonel Anderson had a

lucky escape when he was called to the headquarters of Combat Command B for an important meeting. In order to get there he had to drive through territory not yet liberated by the troops. Anderson took off down a side road, and ran into a small German party. The Germans stopped his jeep, but the lieutenant-colonel and his driver managed to escape capture by ducking into the brush at the side of the road and making their way back to safety on foot later in the day.

Kluge was now beginning to realize that his forces were seriously threatened by Patton's new thrust. On 11 August he sent the commander of the Fifth Panzer Army, Panzer General Heinrich Eberbach, to organize the defence of Alençon. Panzer divisions withdrawn from Mortain were to follow as fast as possible to build up a defensive front against Patton's thrust. Eberbach found only the remnants of 9th Panzer holding the town, including a battalion of infantry, a

■ *Right:* Allied fighter-bombers from Weyland's XIX Tactical Air Command, such as these P-51 Mustangs, wrought havoc on the retreating German columns.

battalion of artillery and a dozen tanks. More than 300 American tanks were motoring relentlessly towards them.

The Luftwaffe was also ordered to throw every aircraft available into the battle to halt Patton's tanks. Time after time, Tactical Air Command fighters had to break off from ground-attack strikes to intercept formations of 20 to 40 German strike aircraft trying to halt the Third Army's spearheads. Weyland now ordered a wave of heavy strikes on German airfields around Paris, which were the source of the trouble, leading to a series of dogfights as the US pilots caught German aircraft returning to their bases. On 7 August, Weyland's men shot down 14 aircraft and destroyed 19 on the ground. This intense battle continued until 11 August, with similar losses being inflicted on the Luftwaffe on a daily basis by Weyland's aircraft. The interdiction

effort against German supply lines continued unabated amid this air battle, with XIX Tactical Air Command claiming 75 locomotives, 1000 railway freight cars, 1000 motor vehicles, 7 bridges, 8 railway marshalling yards, and 8 fuel and ammunition dumps destroyed between 6 and 12 August alone.

The advance of the 5th Armored was much slower during 11 August due to German roadblocks and tank ambushes. Concentrated fire from 105mm and 150mm artillery howitzers was reported for the first time. When Combat Command A came upon the approaches to St-Rémy, French civilians reported that the German armour in the town consisted of 23 tanks and one 88mm gun. Task Force Burton deployed to advance upon the town and received tank fire at ranges greater than 1828m (6000ft). Two artillery battalions were

■ *Above:* US personnel take cover on the Caen-Falaise road during a bombing raid by Allied aircraft.

brought into action to pound the enemy defences. They were joined by the tank destroyers of 628th Tank Destroyer Battalion. Then, after the fighter-bombers gave the town a working-over, infantrymen were sent into the attack. They found that one Panther tank had been destroyed and the Germans had fled.

The 10th Tank Battalion came under fire from Tiger tanks. This enemy armour was subjected to fire from the 81mm mortars and from the guns of the 95th Artillery Battalion. Then air support was called for and the fighter-bombers, peeling off and roaring down on the town, bombed and strafed the enemy positions. Columns of black smoke that spiralled up into the sky indicated several hits. Dismounting from their halftracks, the foot troops

closed in and cleared out the buildings as the armoured column moved through the town. The assault troops assembled for the night on the high ground just north of Essay. But their action for the day was not yet finished. In the darkness, a Tiger tank came creeping back towards the town and was destroyed.

Haislip's troops renewed their advance on 12 August, with a task force of the Free French division dodging past the weak German defence screen to capture key bridges in Alençon intact. To the east, the 5th Armored Division cruised past the town and drove into Sées, which was defended by a German bakery company. The 79th Infantry Division made intensive use of air support to blast through the German defences to its front, calling in P-51

■ *Left:* Caught out in the open, with nowhere to hide, German armour was highly vulnerable to attack from the air and from artillery.

■ *Below:* A US heavy artillery piece pours deadly fire into the Falaise Pocket from its camouflaged position.

Mustangs whenever they encountered enemy resistance.

Realizing that his troops were pushing an open door, Haislip had already expanded his objective to Argentan, where Patton hoped his troops would link up with Canadians advancing down from the north through Falaise. The Canadians were making heavy weather against strong German resistance, though, so Patton visited Haislip and ordered him to push across the boundary between Twelfth and Twenty-First Army Groups, which ran from Vire to Sées. At the same time, however, his Third Army Headquarters was receiving instructions from Bradley's Twelfth Army Group ordering

■ *Above:* **US Third Army soldiers perform house-clearing missions during the Falaise operation.**

the ground troops not to attempt to proceed across the escape corridor. Patton's troops were not supposed to cross this line in case they came under fire by mistake from Montgomery's troops. Ultra reports of chaos and confusion inside the German pocket heavily influenced Patton, though, and he was keen to finish off the trapped troops as fast as possible. "Pay no attention to Monty's goddamn boundaries," Patton told Haislip that evening. "Be prepared to push beyond Falaise."

Closing the Falaise Gap

Haislip urged his divisional commanders to press forward even more relentlessly. The 5th Armored was given the mission of continuing on the way to Argentan, to cut all communications to the north and to help close the Falaise Gap. Its artillery was ordered to to catch any enemy trying to get out the east. Combat Command A was to push northwest, Combat Command Reserve was to move northeast, and Combat Command B was to fill in the gaps to the south and east.

Resistance in front of Combat Command A on the morning of 12 August was very light, and it took Sées by 10:00 hours and then pushed forward. 9th Panzer continued withdrawing, attempting to evacuate its troops to Evreux, Dreux and Bernay. German armour was massing to hold off the 5th Armored's advance, with as many as 200 tanks being reported in its general area. Tanks replaced anti-tank guns at some German roadblocks, showing more tenacious defensive tactics. The 10th Tank Battalion, advancing on the town of Gacé, ran into a well-defended minefield and stalled.

The Free French division soon found its axis of advance towards Carrouges blocked by the huge d'Ecouves forest, which forced the divisional commander, Jacques-Philippe Leclerc, to divert his troops eastwards. The French columns ran into the 5th Armored advancing north from Sées, which forced it to halt its advance for five hours while Leclerc's troops cleared out of the way. Then the American tanks had to wait for fuel tankers to come forward, and only began their attack late in the day to outflank and defeat the 9th Panzer Division. This delay was enough for Eberbach to rush a panzergrenadier battalion of the 116th Panzer Division to Argentan. It arrived in time to repulse the late-evening attack of the 5th Armored's Combat Command A, which allowed the remainder of the 116th Panzer to arrive. The *Leibstandarte* and *Das Reich* Waffen-SS Panzer Divisions were on their way, and Eberbach hoped to launch a concerted counterattack on the following day.

The 5th Armored in action

A self-propelled 75mm assault gun in the column of the 116th Panzer Division was instrumental in holding up the 5th Armored's advance. It destroyed a halftrack and shot the tracks off two tanks. US artillery fire forced the German armour to pull back, and American infantry moved into action to flush out the rearguard. The 5th Armored Division claimed 301 Germans killed and 362 captured, as well as 70 tanks, 88 miscellaneous motor vehicles, 2 armoured cars and 7 pieces of artillery destroyed during the day's advance.

XIX Tactical Air Command's fighter-bombers played an important part in maintaining the rapid rate of advance of XV Corps, but German planes struck back, strafing US columns three times during the day. While German air attacks were a nuisance, they never seriously interfered with Patton's army. Between 6 and 12 August, Weyland's fighter-bomber pilots claimed to have destroyed more than 150 German tanks and armoured cars, as well as 30 field guns or mobile flak posts; scattered 3 troop concentrations; and strafed a headquarters. Under this relentless pounding, it was almost impossible for the Germans to move and concentrate large tank forces in daylight. Allied airpower paralyzed their defences.

Target Argentan

By 19:00 hours on 12 August, the 5th Armored Division was on the edge of Argentan south of the River Orne. Two of the attacking tanks had been knocked out by mines and one had been destroyed by anti-tank gun fire. Not wishing to tangle with the Germans in the darkness, Combat Command A pulled back to the high ground overlooking the town. Large numbers of German tanks and infantry could be seen gathering in Argentan, so two US artillery battalions blasted the town and its approaches. During the night 5th Armored soldiers could hear the mass movement of German vehicles trying to escape eastwards out of the Falaise Pocket. Many of these clanking enemy columns crashed into the American roadblocks and were destroyed or captured as they tried to flee. The artillery pieces continued to pour deadly fire into the pocket.

Early on the morning of 13 August, Combat Command A resumed its attack northwards. It met with strong resistance and was repulsed. During the night the enemy had moved in more infantry and anti-tank guns to guard the town. Deadly 88mm flak guns were placed in concealed positions on the flanks and on the dominating ground to the north of the town, which knocked out seven Sherman tanks of the 34th Tank Battalion and severely injured its commanding officer. CCA then tried to smash its way into the town from the south, but could not get through a line of massed panzer tanks on the outskirts of the city. Supporting fire from the artillery and

fighter-bombers did not help greatly in whittling down these defences, because the German tanks were well concealed in and among the buildings near the railroad marshalling yards.

The combat command's reserve was then sent around the right flank to cut the road to Gacé, but the Germans threw in 35 Panther tanks and successfully resisted all efforts to push north of Argentan. At noon the 628th Tank Destroyer Battalion was sent to reinforce the attack. As the combat command staff made plans for another attack that afternoon, the reconnaissance platoon of the 34th Tank Battalion kept a watchful eye on the town. It observed the Germans laying down a hasty minefield on the edge of Argentan. But before another attack got under way, orders were received stating that the 2nd French Armoured Division would take over the mission to seize Argentan from the southwest.

At this point orders were changed, cancelled and then reissued. Orders were also received from XV Corps to send a combat command up the Argentan-Falaise highway, in an attempt to join the Canadians at Falaise. This plan was also changed before it could be put into effect.

Patton is ordered to halt

There was difficulty obtaining permission from Montgomery to cross the army group boundary. Bradley was still nominally subordinate to the British general, who was Allied land forces commander until Eisenhower's headquarters was properly up and running. Just after midday on 13 August, Bradley met up with Montgomery to finalize arrangements for the encirclement of Falaise. The following day the Canadians were due to launch a deliberate attack with heavy bomber support to blast through the German lines and allow them to storm

■ *Above:* French townspeople gather around a US truck containing German prisoners. Thousands of Wehrmacht and SS troops were captured or killed as the Allies closed the Falaise Gap.

into Falaise. At the same time, Patton was to bring up another corps to swing to the east of XV Corps and close the Falaise Pocket. So Patton was ordered to halt Haislip's advance, and at 14:15 hours on 13 August he ordered XV Corps to stop and pull its troops back from Argentan. The prospect of the flanking movement excited Patton and mollified him to a certain extent over the failure to close the Falaise Gap.

As part of the move, the 5th Armored was ordered to prevent German use of the roads leading east from Argentan, being careful not to be dragged into a fight for the city itself. In addition, it would also cut roads leading out of Gacé to the east.

The Free French had now finally cleared the Forest of Ecouves and captured Carrouges. Leclerc then ordered his troops to push on to Argentan, and by the afternoon they were in the centre of town to the applause of grateful citizens. Liberation did not last long, though, as the 116th Panzer Division's 15 tanks arrived and drove out the French soldiers. The 5th Armored tried to outflank Argentan to the east, only to run into dug-in German anti-tank guns and tanks which brought its advance to a halt. Now Eberbach's reinforcements arrived, but he was forced to use them to build up a defensive line rather than strike at the superior US and French forces.

Desperate German troops try to ferry themselves to safety at Rouen following their escape from the Falaise Gap. The arrows indicate German barges.

Patton was still pleading with Bradley for permission to launch a concerted push north of Argentan. "We now have elements in Argentan," he said. "Shall we continue and drive the British into the sea for another Dunkirk?" Ultra reported that the German withdrawal from the pocket was gathering pace, and Patton believed his troops had the strength to punch past the weak German defences and link up with the Canadians, some 32km (20 miles) to the north, to trap the Germans before they escaped westwards.

Bradley was not so confident that Patton's men could withstand the fury of 200,000 heavily armed and desperate Germans trying to fight their way to freedom, stating his preference for "a solid shoulder at Argentan to the possibility of a broken neck at Falaise". XV Corps at this point was separated from First Army's nearest unit by some 40km (25 miles) of open flank, which Bradley thought was highly vulnerable to a German counterattack until US troops closed it late on 13 August.

Bradley said he thought Patton's suggestion would have been a "dangerous and uncontrollable manoeuvre". The inability to properly coordinate artillery fire and air support if the US and Canadian forces advanced too quickly was also given by Bradley as a reason to halt XV Corps.

During 13 August, the fighter-bombers and artillery continued hammering targets in the vicinity of Argentan. One severely mauled enemy column, which decided to abandon its attempt to run this gauntlet out of the slowly closing trap, signalled its desire to surrender to aircraft of the US 511st Fighter Squadron by waving 300 to 400 white flags. An order was dropped by the airmen to the commander of the

■ *Right:* As the Allied troops made their way through the battlefields of Falaise, they encountered thousands of dead soldiers and animals, as well as smashed armour.

column, which directed him to march his troops to Rodeau. This column grew to 17,000 Wehrmacht soldiers and surrendered to the 90th Infantry Division two days later. XIX Tactical Air Command claimed more than 1000 road and rail vehicles, 45 tanks and other armoured vehicles and 12 locomotives destroyed on this day alone. Some 10 close air-support strikes were also flown against German positions engaging XV Corps troops.

The 5th Armored's patrols, which had been probing the German defences in Argentan during the night, were withdrawn from the city at daylight on 14 August. Then, at 06:30 hours, a shattering artillery barrage was put down on the city as the enemy troops and vehicles continued their frenzied rush to pass through the city and out of the pocket. They were harassed, too, by the fighter-bombers, which began another

day of bombing and strafing the terror-ridden corridor. Confusion now became general among the German forces in this area. Enemy columns of from five to fifty vehicles, all trying desperately to find their way out of the encirclement, were reported in all sections of the 5th Armored Division's zone. In addition, 10 German tanks were repulsed when they attempted to charge straight through the division's positions just north of Sées. And at 10:30 hours a column of enemy infantry and tanks was bombed in front of the 5th Armored and 79th Infantry Divisions.

Then, at 22:00 hours that evening, orders came down from higher head-quarters to the 5th Armoured Division. Its mission at the Falaise Gap was finished. It was now instructed to be ready to drive east to cross the River Eure and continue to the River Seine, west of Paris.

■ *Above:* Canadian engineers search for mines along the grass verge as they enter Falaise. Mine clearance was one of the prime duties of Allied "sapper" units.

It took the Canadians and their supporting Polish troops two more days to batter their way into Falaise. Inside the ever-diminishing pocket, or *kessel*, meaning "kettle", as the Germans called it, conditions were getting desperate for the Wehrmacht and Waffen-SS troops. Allied bombers and artillery were hitting the German lines incessantly. Wrecked vehicles, dead horses and human corpses were strewn everywhere. Although elements of 23 German divisions were inside the pocket, they were mere ghost units. Each could typically muster only a couple of thousand fighting men and the panzer divisions were lucky to have a dozen tanks in fighting order.

On top of this, Hitler was still insisting that Kluge and Hausser relaunch their offensive towards Avranches. When Kluge told him this was madness, Hitler was furious and the field marshal was soon sacked. The paranoid Hitler became convinced that Kluge was trying to negotiate a surrender with the Allies when he went incommunicado inside the pocket for several hours on 15 August. Kluge, in fact, spent the whole time in a ditch after his staff car had been strafed by Allied fighter-bombers. When Hitler demanded Kluge return to Berlin to explain himself, the field marshal took his own life rather than risk arrest on treason charges. Hitler dispatched Field Marshal Walter Model, an Eastern Front veteran, to take over command of the German forces in Normandy. He did not arrive until 19 August and, in the meantime, command devolved to Hausser, who was the senior officer in the pocket. With communications to Berlin failing, Hausser took matters into his own hands on 18 August and ordered a break-out. Waffen-SS panzer

units would hold open the shoulders of the corridor for as long as possible.

Closing the Falaise Gap

Bradley waited a day before deciding what to do. Montgomery had declared that he still wanted his troops to close the Falaise Gap and that Patton's troops should be used to execute a "wide envelopment" along the Seine. Patton now managed to persuade Bradley to let him strike for the Seine, so he left two divisions holding the "shoulder" of the gap at Argentan and used the remainder of his forces to drive eastwards.

With his hands tied by the stop order, Patton turned to the only combat power available to strike into the pocket: XIX Tactical Air Command. Otto Weyland's pilots staged a maximum effort to hit escaping German columns. On 17 August a huge German column was spotted by one of Weyland's squadrons trying to make its escape in daylight. According to the command's history, "The Germans figured that low cloud was a reasonably good safeguard against our aircraft and they began to take to the roads two and three abreast in anything that had wheels. A squadron of American fighter-bombers dived dangerously low through the clouds and saw the traffic jam. They got word back to headquarters and soon the sky was so full of British and American fighter-bombers that they had to form queues to make their bomb runs. The gigantic offensive kept up until after nightfall."

The following day Weyland's Thunderbolts found a 1500-vehicle convoy and then another 1000 were found nearby. The first column was pounded relentlessly by XIX Tactical Air Command, but the US flyers were

■ *Left:* **Patton liked to use Weyland's fighter-bombers to clear any resistance rather than risk his armour. As this image shows, Weyland's aircraft were deadly.**

disappointed when the RAF refused to let the Americans join the attack on the second column because it was north of the army group boundary line. It eventually turned out to contain 7000 vehicles and the British managed to destroy 3000 of them.

Northwest France beckons

Patton's troops were now advancing in four directions over a huge area of northwestern France. VIII Corps was still engaged in Brittany, although Patton was arguing with Bradley for infantry divisions to release the 4th and 6th Armored Divisions for use in the east. XV Corps was engaged around Argentan. XII Corps had passed through Avranches and was heading for Le Mans, while XX Corps was advancing south from Avranches towards Nantes and Angers on the River Loire. LeRoy Irwin's 5th Infantry Division was spearheading its advance south in trucks. There was nothing blocking its advance but a few scattered groups of German stragglers. When resistance was encountered, US fighter-bombers were called up to deal with them. In one memorable incident, German artillery mounted on a train tried to stop the 5th Infantry Division. Within 45 minutes a squadron of Thunderbolts was overhead and put two 500lb bombs onto the target. The advance rolled on. Angers had fallen on 11 August without a shot being fired, but the XX Corps commander was impatient for the northern bank of the Loire to be secured and he ordered Irwin to rush a battalion westwards to seize Nantes. They got there a few hours later and threw a ring around the city. Walker was soon up with the point troops and ordered an immediate attack. Some 2000 demoralized Germans surrendered as soon as the first GIs probed their defences. Patton's southern flank was now secure. The 5th Infantry was then

■ Above: The view from an Allied reconnaissance aircraft as it sweeps across the Falaise battlefield.

ordered to move northeast towards Le Mans and Chartres, but its route kept being changed on the basis of information from Ultra to ensure it bypassed German rearguards, much to the chagrin of Irwin, who could not be let into the code-breaking secrets.

On 15 August XV Corps turned its attention eastwards, with 5th Armor and the 79th Infantry heading to Dreux. The 90th Infantry swung behind the Free French to take over the key le Bourg–St-Leonard sector, where the head of the pocket was at its narrowest. An open ridge above the village dominated the German escape route out of the pocket, overlooking the valley of the River Divas. As Hausser began moving his troops out of the pocket on 16 August, he dispatched one of his last tank units to drive the 90th Infantry off

its hill. The Germans held the ridge for 24 hours until the 90th Infantry with tank support drove them off. In this time tens of thousands of Germans were able to make their escape.

Montgomery's troops were now past Falaise and heading south, so he asked Bradley to attack northwards from Argentan to close the pocket at Chambois. Haislip, however, had long gone and there was no corps headquarters on hand to coordinate the offensive. Patton had to dispatch his chief of staff, Hugh Gaffey, with an ad hoc command team to lead the attack. The 80th Infantry Division was also ordered to Chambois to support the attack.

Gaffey arrived late on 16 August and had soon issued his attack orders. Meanwhile, Bradley had ordered Major-General Leonard Gerow's V Corps to

■ *Right*: Despite the loss of thousands of tanks, artillery pieces, trucks and men, many thousands more Germans managed to escape before the pocket was finally sealed.

move to take over the attack. Gerow arrived in the Argentan sector early the following morning, but it took him several hours to find Gaffey, so the attack never really got started. A delay in bringing V Corps' heavy guns forward put back the attack date to 18 August.

This attack met with furious resistance from the Germans, who were fighting desperately to hold open a corridor out of the pocket. The 80th Division managed finally to secure a firm foothold in Argentan, but it could not find a way past 88mm flak guns that knocked out American Shermans on the open hillside. Farther east, the 90th Infantry got halfway to Chambois until it became bogged down in heavy fighting in a hellish forest set on fire by artillery shells.

With Allied troops pressing in on the pocket from three sides, the German retreat gathered pace amid the carnage. The 80th and 90th Divisions returned to the attack on 19 August, only to meet even more fanatical resistance. Free French tanks were now committed to the attack on Chambois, and a gap was

finally opened in the German line to allow a link-up with Polish troops advancing southwards.

The ring around the pocket was far from sealed, and during the night of 19/20 August tens of thousands of German troops rushed past the Allied troops at Chambois. For the next two days the battle raged as Allied troops tried to seal all escape routes and neutralize the last pockets of resistance. Artillery and air strikes raked the pocket.

There was no formal surrender or break-out. The scene Allied troops found as they combed the ruins of the German Army in Normandy was truly apocalyptic. They found 567 tanks, 950 artillery pieces, 7700 vehicles and the bodies of 10,000 Germans and the carcasses of tens of thousands of horses. Some 50,000 Germans surrendered, and 20,000 others made their escape on foot. Of the 38 German divisions in Normandy, 25 had ceased to exist. The German Army had lost almost 500,000 men since 6 June 1944, and was in headlong retreat.

CHAPTER 6

DRIVE TO THE SEINE

"To attack with the limited forces I have available – since I occupy a [480km] 300-mile front [and had lost XV Corps to Hodges] – I am taking chances, but I am convinced that the situation in the German Army warrants the taking of such risks."
Patton, mid-August 1944

As the battle to destroy the German armies in the Falaise Pocket was entering its terminal phase, Patton had his eyes trained farther east. Like Montgomery, Patton was convinced that large German forces had escaped from Normandy and were trying to escape across the River Seine to set up a new defensive line.

Patton thought it was essential to keep up the pressure on the retreating Germans and make sure they kept retreating all the way back to their Reich. The Third Army was about to embark on one of its most dramatic advances, which would take it to the gates of Paris.

On the evening of 13 August, Patton was still smarting at Bradley's orders to halt his push to close the Falaise Gap at Argentan. "My only worries are my relations, not my enemies," commented Patton. Denied his chance to destroy the Germans at Falaise, Patton turned his attention to striking eastwards, with the towns of Dreux and Chartres his immediate objectives.

■ *Left:* **Third Army armour rolls into Dreux on its way to liberate Paris in August 1944. Abandoned German equipment, including a PAK 38 anti-tank gun (right), litters the road. The light vehicle on the left is a US Army jeep.**

The following morning, he flew to see Bradley and proposed his plan. XV Corps would hold the "shoulder" of the Falaise Pocket at Argentan, while the bulk of Wade Haislip's force struck directly eastwards to Dreux, XX Corps struck east for Chartres and XII Corps headed for Orléans. Ultra told Patton that the Germans were in shock after the envelopment of the Falaise Pocket, and were struggling to prepare their defences between the Seine and Loire rivers. They had to be hit hard in the next few days to prevent them establishing a firm front, said Patton.

After a strong sales pitch from Patton, Bradley decided to give the Third Army commander his head. He also agreed to release the 6th Armored Division from Brittany to join the Third Army's offensive.

Montgomery had a rival plan to close the Falaise Pocket by dropping an airborne division on Dreux and Chartres, right in the path of Patton's armoured spearheads. This spurred the American general to get there first.

An excited Patton rushed back to his command post and had his staff issue the necessary orders. The attack was timed to start at 20:30 hours that evening to make use of the long summer nights, and to prevent Bradley changing his mind or Montgomery countermanding the orders. Not content with the limited objectives given by Bradley,

■ *Above:* After receiving permission from Bradley to push on to the Seine, Patton (left) set about organizing his army with a vengeance.

Patton warned his corps commanders that they were soon likely to be ordered to push on to the Seine. He also alerted his logistic planners to start moving up the necessary supplies to keep the advance going way beyond the Seine.

The first of Patton's corps to move was Haislip's north of Alençon, and just after 21:00 hours RAF fighter-bombers patrolling west of Dreux were very surprised to find a column of tanks heading towards the town. It was the 79th Division's reconnaissance troops that had moved out during the evening.

Other units of XV Corps received orders later that evening for movement early on 15 August. The 5th Armored Division's new mission was to proceed east to seize a line of the River Seine between Meulan and Vernon. Elements of the Waffen-SS *Leibstandarte* and *Das Reich* Panzer Divisions were identified by Ultra intelligence near Dreux, and a concentration of tanks, infantry and artillery was reported at Chartres, along with regiments of the German 331st Infantry Division, elements of the 116th Panzer Division and two other panzer divisions. The 17th Luftwaffe Field Division was moving across the Seine, after arriving from Holland to block XV Corps' route of advance.

Advance on Dreux

During the day the 90th Infantry Division relieved the 5th Armored in the Argentan-Gacé sector, and Lunsford Oliver's tanks started on their new mission late in the afternoon. During the march, maintenance of radio communications was very difficult due to enemy interference and unfavourable terrain. On numerous occasions the combat commands lost contact with heads of columns, which made control difficult. Enemy resistance on all routes was light, consisting mostly of roadblocks. These were not strongly defended, though, and only occasionally were anti-tank guns encountered. The Germans were in the process of withdrawing towards Dreux, and when the 5th Armored prepared to attack they found strong German tank forces and anti-tank defences. XIX Tactical Air Command put its élite rocket-armed fighter squadron, the 513th, into the air to support the 5th Armored. The "Tiger taming" outfit claimed the destruction of four German

■ *Below:* Sherman tanks of the Third Army advance across country in mid-August 1944. Note the infantry riding on the tank to the left. Though a potentially dangerous ride, it was better than walking!

heavy tanks with its 5in rocket-armed ground-attack aircraft.

German planes were also active, strafing the XV Corps columns during the day in 12-strong formations, but American fighters intervened to drive them off. Oliver pushed his men to advance forward during the late summer evening until the light was gone.

The 5th Armored struck at Dreux during the afternoon of 16 August. The first of its task forces to approach the town was engaged by four dug-in 88mm flak guns, which knocked out one M3 light tank, and then accurate German artillery fire started to land amid the assault columns.

A platoon of German Panzer IV medium tanks then ambushed another US task force trying to enter Dreux from the north side of town. US M7 105mm self-propelled guns, firing over open sights, eventually drove off the

Germans and allowed the attack to roll forward again. The 5th Armored's history records the details of the battle:

"The mission fell to Task Force Giorlando. The plan called for the offensive to bear down on the town from the wooded approaches to the south; it would straddle the main highway, with the 15th Infantry Battalion's 'A' Company on the right and 'C' Company on the left. Each company would be supported by a light tank platoon from 'D' Company, 81st Tank Battalion. The attacking companies would also be supported by fire from the field pieces of the 71st Artillery Battalion, and by the Assault Gun Platoon advancing along the highway.

"Defending the town was a battalion of German infantrymen. They were well concealed along the edge of the woods on the south side of the town. They also had two anti-tank guns in position with

■ *Below:* **US armour and infantry take on a German machine-gun nest on the road to Coudray. Cooperation between armour and infantry was crucial to the success of the Third Army in France.**

the barrels pointed straight down the main highway.

"These Wehrmacht soldiers lay quietly and made no move as the line of 'A' and 'C' Company 'doughs' [the nickname for GIs originally used in World War I] trudged slowly and cautiously toward the town. Then when the attack wave had approached to within a few hundred yards of the trees the forest suddenly erupted in an outpouring of machine-gun, rifle and anti-tank fire. Stunned by this surprise blow, the dazed GIs were thrown back and two halftracks of the Assault Gun Platoon were destroyed.

"Lieutenants Polim and Isaacs quickly reorganized their platoons and

then, with supporting fire from the tanks, artillery, and assault guns, both companies again rushed the woods. This time they rolled over the enemy's defences. With direct fire Lieutenant Melvin Abbott's Assault Gun Platoon knocked out the two anti-tank guns. As the attack pushed through the woods and continued on toward the town, a German soldier, who was a member of the medical corps, came forward and offered to surrender 500 Germans in the town. Colonel Cole told the man he would be given a half hour to bring the garrison out of Dreux. Then the task force held its fire and waited, but after the half hour had ticked away and no Germans emerged from the town, the

■ *Above:* A GI inspects a destroyed German 88mm anti-tank gun on the road to Orléans. Note the German mines in the centre foreground.

attack was resumed. When the GIs reached the built-up sections of Dreux they found that the cagey Germans had withdrawn to a cemetery and were shelling the houses with mortars and artillery. But this final opposition was soon overcome and by 17:15 hours the town was in the hands of the Task Force. The happy inhabitants of Dreux then came out of their basements and other places of shelter and gave the 5th Armored troops a loud and joyous welcome."

The impact of airpower

Another German battalion managed to escape from the town and retreat across the River Eure, pursued by the 5th Armored's Reconnaissance Squadron. One company of German tanks was spotted organizing a counterattack but the division engaged them, damaging 7 out of 30 tanks.

XIX Tactical Air Command ensured its fighter-bombers were always in the air over the 5th Armored. It reported: "The night of Dreux, eight P-47s flying armoured column cover were vectored to a road junction where anti-tank guns and infantry were holding up the advance. Our Thunderbolts attacked it with six 500lb bombs, four frag[mentation] clusters and strafing. Results were not observed, but the ground force indicated the guns were destroyed and they congratulated the squadron leader."

During the afternoon of 17 August, the 5th Armored was ordered to seize a crossing over the Eure for the use of the 2nd French Armored Division in case it had to be released to attack Paris. German resistance was still stubbornly holding the Eure line to allow their troops to continue their withdrawal from the Falaise Pocket.

The quick capture of Dreux and the Eure crossings on 16 August made it unnecessary for the Allies to mount the large-scale airborne operation to take

bridgeheads on the east bank of the river between Dreux and Chartres. This had been scheduled to begin on 18 August.

The assault on Orléans

Gilbert Cook's XII Corps was moving into Le Mans when the new orders arrived during the evening, so they were not in a position to attack until the morning of 15 August. John Wood's 4th Armored Division had just arrived in the town after a long drive from Brittany and was in the process of refuelling. Cook quickly sent it on its way westwards after Patton telephoned the XII Corps commander to complain about the division's slow progress. Ultra had indicated to Patton that the German garrison in Orléans had been ordered to evacuate, so there was no time to lose.

Wood formed an ad hoc task force drawn from both divisions and dispatched them down the main road to Orléans, with Bruce Clarke's Combat Command A in the lead. P-47 Thunderbolts ranged ahead of Clarke's column, strafing any German vehicles they found. Patton commented, "just east of Le Mans was one of the best examples of armor and air cooperation I have ever seen. For about two miles the road was full of enemy motor transport and armor, many of which bore the unmistakable calling card of a P-47 fighter-bomber – namely a group of .50-caliber holes."

The American force had to find fords across rivers blocking their route after finding the Germans had demolished the main bridges. Having reached the outskirts of Orléans by dark, they then stormed a large Luftwaffe fighter airfield heavily fortified with anti-tank and anti-aircraft guns. Colonel Clarke then quickly prepared his troops to attack the historic city, with his tanks swinging north and the troops of Paul Baade's 35th Infantry Division assaulting from

■ *Above:* US infantry and armour continue the fight into Orléans itself. The magnificent cathedral in the background was severely damaged in World War II, along with much of old Orléans.

the west. This pincer attack quickly overwhelmed the small German garrison and soon Joan of Arc's city was liberated. The divisional history of the 35th "Sante Fe" Infantry recorded the attack on the historic city:

"The Germans used Orléans as the seat for the occupational forces in this section of France. Here they had built a great airfield and stored vast supplies. Le Mans to Orléans is approximately [128 kilometers] 80 miles. The breakthrough to the south was complete. Confusion reigned in the German ranks. Now, with the River Loire as right flank protection, General

Patton was ready to change direction and strike in Blitzkrieg fashion to the east. With only a road map to guide them, the 'Santa Fe' was ordered to capture Orléans.

"Morale was high as the division began to roll. Task Force 'S,' commanded by Brigadier-General Edmond Sebree (the divisional assistant commander, and consisting of Combat Team 137, Company D, 737th Tank Battalion, Company B and Reconnaissance Company of the 654th Tank Destroyer Battalion, and the 127th Field Artillery Battalion) was selected by General Baade to lead. Later Combat

■ *Left:* The joyful people of Orléans display the "V for victory" sign, so famously popularized by British prime minister Winston Churchill, after being liberated by Patton's men.

■ *Right:* Tanks of the US Third Army outside Chartres. The action on the outskirts of the town was uneventful and routine.

Command A of the 4th Armored Division was attached to the 35th and spearheaded this attack. General Sebree began the movement in the direction of Orléans at 11:00 hours on 15 August. Tanks of the 4th and doughboys of the 35th formed in a great team and swept aside all opposition. Literally, they raced down the fine French highway. Thirty hours later they stood before Orléans itself as a new page was written in the Blitzkrieg book.

"Much evidence appeared along the road which showed the loss of equipment suffered by the enemy. Burned and overturned German tanks, guns, trucks, trailers, and other items of warfare were strewn along the countryside. In several places complete motor pools had been destroyed as the Allied airmen raked the countryside ahead of the dashing ground forces. As the Task Force closed in upon Orléans, the 2nd and 3rd Battalions of the 137th were on the north while the 1st was pushing south to the Loire. Some resistance was encountered in the woods between Coulmiers and Ormes and casualties were suffered at this point.

■ *Right:* More Third Army armour on the outskirts of Chartres. Though the advance into the town was easy, once inside the town the US forces met with determined resistance.

■ **Above: US
infantry from
Patton's Third Army
look on into
Chartres as
artillery softens
up the German
positions.**

"As the advance continued through Ormes, a suburb of Orléans, a large German warehouse was captured which contained a complete stock of new kitchen equipment as well as a large supply of motor fuel. A machine shop was also found stocked with airplane motors and other ordnance. Pushing into Orléans, the 137th's 2nd Battalion reached the railroad crossing on the Ormes highway at 13:00 hours on 16 August. Two hours later the 3rd Battalion was in the northwest part of the city and at 19:00 hours the City Hall was captured."

In the meantime, on 15/16 August the other units of the 35th were also having a field day. Combat Teams 134 and 320 were dashing down the Orléans highway. The 134th advanced

to the vicinity of Binas Verdas where, in addition to being in reserve, they patrolled and cleaned out enemy stragglers in the rear areas and guarded the Santa Fe's line of communications.

As Combat Team 320 was ready to proceed down the Le Mans–Orléans road during the evening of 15 August, its mission was suddenly changed. Châteaudun, 64km (40 miles) to the northwest of Orléans, was now the objective. Throughout the night the unit rolled on. The next morning as they advanced from Veray, heavy small-arms, mortar, artillery and rocket fire fell among them. But the dauntless 320th pressed the attack, and by noon on 17 August Châteaudun fell. In addition, the 320th captured the bypassed town of Cloyes. The frontline

■ *Above:* German prisoners taken by XII Corps await transportation to POW camps to sit out the rest of the war. Some were probably relieved it was all over.

of the Santa Fe was at this moment 64km (40 miles) long!

In Orléans, despite machine-gun and heavy artillery fire from German positions across the River Loire and a constant sniper menace, there were very few casualties suffered by the Task Force. During the night, occupation of the city was completed and by morning all hostile resistance had withdrawn across the river. The Germans had, however, left dynamite, bombs and other explosives in the post office, the

telephone building and other places. The bridge across the Loire was destroyed along with the water mains, cutting off the city's water supply. But the 60th Engineers saved the situation by supplying from 60,000 to 80,000 gallons of water per day to the citizens.

The citizenry went wild with joy at the quick and expeditious manner in which the Germans had been ousted. Apparently the decision to withdraw had been a hasty one. They had pulled out of the *Feldcommandatur 589* so

quickly that the staff had left soup and stew uneaten on the dinner table, and there was warm soapy water in the bathtub. This headquarters was later occupied by General Sebree, and *Feldcommandatur* was changed to "Santa Fe".

It appeared, with all their reputation for thoroughness, that the jittery Nazis had neglected to notify all of their army agencies of the evacuation. A German airman, unaware that the city was in American hands, attempted to land at the airfield north of the city and was shot down when he tried to make a last-minute getaway. Many valuable maps and documents were found intact, and a vast amount of military intelligence was culled from these. Much information was also obtained from the Free French and the *Maquis* (French Resistance fighters) who met the Americans as they entered the city.

■ *Above:* A German halftrack knocked out by the 813th Tank Destroyer Unit of the US 79th Infantry Division.

Though the Germans were still across the river and occasionally sent machine-gun and artillery fire into Orléans, the happy citizens considered the city freed and had a great celebration. On 17 August the American leaders were notified at 09:40 hours that their presence was requested at the festivities, which were to take place at 10:00 hours. General Sebree, Colonel Ellsworth of Division Artillery, Colonel Sears, Commanding Officer of the 137th Infantry Regiment, and 2nd Lieutenant Anders N. Kullander, aide to General Sebree, attended. The delirious crowds paraded through the streets carrying banners of the Allied nations with signs proclaiming the slogans of Allied victory. Thousands along the way shouted their enthusiastic greeting to the American soldiers.

Ecstasy in Orléans

The parade moved down the Rue de la Republique to the Statue of the Maid of Orléans at the city's centre. The buildings around the square had been demolished and even the base of the statue was damaged. The statue itself, however, was untouched.

The newly appointed Commissioner for the Republic, M. André Mars, introduced the American officers, each of whom made a few appropriate remarks. The ceremonies ended with the singing of the great song of French liberty, *La Marseillaise*, while the crowd threw flowers at the statue.

At 14:00 hours on the 17th the Germans again began to shell the city from across the river, but General Sebree sent the following message to General Baade through Major Clarence E. Woods, Assistant G-2: "I am neither confused nor confounded. I can hold the city against two divisions – not against two corps, but two divisions."

The 4th Armored's Combat Command B was also advancing along the north bank of the Loire from Nantes, clearing up small pockets of German resistance and forcing them to blow up several bridges across the river. When the 4th Armored came under XII Corps on 15 August, Lorient was left to the 6th Armored Division and John Wood's troops began their longest continuous march. The columns drove east 422km (264 miles) in 34 hours before halting at Prunay, south of Vendôme. A small task force, with the mission of destroying bridges, engaged in a bizarre battle across the gentle valley of the Loire River. The US column, commanded by Major Edward Bautz, was moving on the north bank near Amboise when it located a German column on the opposite bank. The GIs opened fire with everything from machine guns to 75mm cannons, inflicting heavy losses on the Germans who were trapped between high ground and the river.

The rapid advance of XII Corps effectively unhinged the German Army's position south of Paris, and prevented them forming a new defensive line between Paris and Orléans.

The battle for Chartres

XX Corps, meanwhile, under Walton Walker, had been delayed by traffic jams in Le Mans caused by the presence of XII Corps' logistic vehicles waiting to move east after their lead elements, which were heading towards Orléans. Walker had been assigned the 7th Armored Division, which had just motored to Le Mans after landing at Omaha beach in Normandy on 7 August. By the afternoon of 13 August it was assembling east of Le Mans. Even though the division was not yet complete, Walter ordered it into action immediately and early the next day three columns were moving on Dreux. They had hardly got into their stride when new orders arrived, changing their

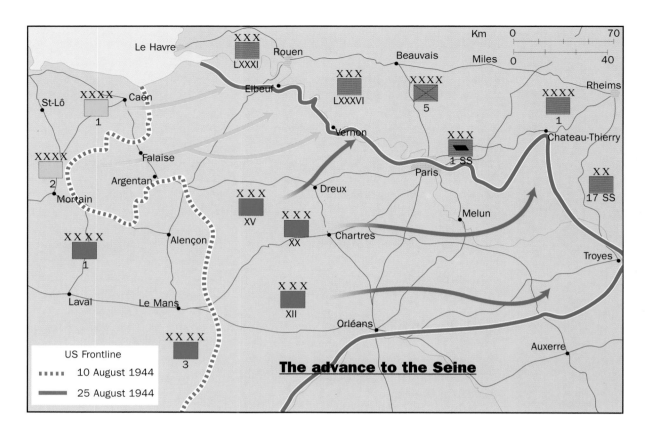

The advance to the Seine

objective to Chartres. Reports from Ultra of German supply problems in the region made Patton keen to take the town, which he presumed was weakly held by the enemy.

Although the advance to the outskirts of Chartres on 15 August was relatively uneventful, the US troops then ran into determined German resistance. Finding themselves vulnerable to small groups of German troops armed with Panzerfausts (anti-tank rockets), the US tanks pulled back to reorganize for a daytime attack. A German ambush of a column from Company "B" of the 23rd Armored Infantry Battalion at the town of Marbouén, near Chartres, on the evening of 15 August, destroyed seven halftracks and a jeep and caused heavy casualties.

Holding Chartres was an ad hoc battlegroup centred on a Luftwaffe flak training centre, and they put up a fierce fight when the 7th Armored attacked on 16 August. The Americans managed to secure a toehold in the town but the Sherman crews found it difficult to man- oeuvre in the narrow streets, making them vulnerable to German tank-killing teams. Even though elements of XX Corps' artillery were brought up to support 7th Armored, the American attack stalled. Walker now ordered up the 5th Infantry Division to support his tanks. It took a whole day for the infantry to move forward and get ready, so the XX Corps attack did not go in until 18 August. In a day of heavy fighting, the 7th and 5th Divisions swept into the town and eventually broke all resistance. Some 2000 Ger- mans surrendered and a huge airfield complete with 50 aircraft was captured.

On the northern wing of the Third Army, XV Corps had seized Dreux against negligible opposition by the afternoon of 16 August. The 79th Infantry Division had driven 96km (60 miles) forward along open roads to

■ *Above:* In the two weeks from 10 August the Third Army advanced on a broad front towards the River Seine, forcing the German evacuation of Paris.

Nogent-le-Roi on the same day and reported "no contact with the enemy". Haislip was then told to be prepared to push on to the Seine at Mantes-Gassicourt. Even before the towns of Orléans and Chartres had fallen, Patton was urging Bradley to allow him to push forward to the Seine. Patton was keen to maintain the momentum of his advance and take Paris, while at the same time swinging north along the Seine valley north of the French capital to trap the German forces that had escaped from the Falaise Pocket.

When Bradley arrived at Patton's headquarters on the morning of 15 August, he was initially not keen to allow the Third Army to move too far ahead of the main US and British forces, in case the Germans turned on it. There were also growing problems supplying Patton's columns with enough fuel to maintain their rapid rate of advance, even when transport aircraft were drafted in to fly fuel for his tanks to forward airstrips.

Patton strains at the leash

Patton was incensed when Bradley ordered him to halt along a line Dreux-Chartres-Orléans. In typical Patton fashion, he told Bradley he had just returned from XV Corps where he boasted that he had "pissed in the Seine" and wondered if he wanted the Third Army to retreat? In fact, Haislip's spearheads were several miles from the river, but Patton did not want that to undermine his argument. For two days, Bradley and Montgomery pondered what to do and kept Patton's troops stationary to allow them to be resupplied. One consolation for Patton was that on 16 August he was at last allowed to go public and drop the pretence that he was still in England preparing to invade the Pas-de-Calais. Patton declared that the Third Army could now claim its rightful share of the glory for the defeat of the Germans in the Normandy campaign.

In the meantime, using Ultra intercepts, Patton now unleashed XIX Tactical Air Command's fighter-bombers against the bridges and ferries the Germans were using to move their troops back across the Seine. At the same time, XIX Tactical Air Command was busy relocating its bases forward and established a large base at the airfield at Châteaudun, which only a few days before had been home to a huge Luftwaffe base.

Crisis at the top

This was a time of great tension among the Allied High Command in Normandy over the conduct of the final defeat of the German forces escaping from Falaise. Patton was fuming at Bradley and, in his diary, accused his superior of "suffering from nerves". Just at this point the Free French government began insisting that its 2nd Armoured Division be released from its mission of closing the Falaise Gap at Argentan to spearhead the liberation of Paris. Its commander, Jacques-Philippe Leclerc, lobbied Patton on a daily basis to be allowed to move on his capital. He had several stormy meetings with Patton until the Third Army commander told him to stop behaving "like a baby". General Charles de Gaulle, the Free French leader, had now intervened with Eisenhower to ensure that Leclerc's men got the job of freeing Paris.

While Patton and his men kicked their heels between Dreux and Orléans, Eisenhower, Bradley and Montgomery were working to craft an Allied strategy to advance to the Seine. Patton was to be allowed to unleash his columns to push south and north of Paris to secure bridgeheads across the Seine. At a meeting on 17 August, Bradley carved up the "zones of action" for their armies with Hodges and Patton. He was also to use his XV Corps to spearhead a flanking move northwards along the Seine towards Rouen to cut off the retreating German columns from Falaise. Leclerc got his wish to lead the advance on Paris, but he would not be under Patton's command. Courtney Hodges' First Army would have that honour. Patton wrote that night, "Unless I get the stop order in the next two hours, we are jumping again. On paper it looks risky but I don't think so." Patton knew from Ultra and Weyland's air patrols that the roads eastwards were open.

XII Corps strikes

First off the starting blocks was XV Corps, which headed for Mantes-Gassicourt on 18 August, while XX Corps aimed to hit the Seine south of Paris, and XII Corps was directed to Sens. The latter corps now had a new commander, Manton Eddy, because Cook had been relieved by Patton after he was hospitalized with circulation problems in his legs. Eddy had been promoted from commanding the 9th Infantry Division, which had suffered heavily in the Normandy Bocage fighting. There, on a good day, he measured his success in terms of a few hundred meters advanced. On the first day in charge of XII Corps Patton ordered him to advance 112km (70 miles) from Orléans to Sens and not worry about his unprotected flanks. Patton reported that Eddy turned pale when he heard his orders.

South of Paris, the German First Army was in hopeless disarray and there were few organized combat units, only scattered logistic, garrison and security units. Reports from Ultra painted a picture of weak German forces

■ *Right:* A US trooper uses a bridge in Chartres as a spotting point for two Browning machine guns.

desperately trying to pull themselves together into a coherent defence line. Patton was determined not to let this happen, though.

With 4th Armored Division in the lead, XII Corps headed for Sens at breakneck speed. When the division's advance guard reached the River Loire and found the Germans had blown the main road bridge, they quickly discovered a usable bridge 24km (15 miles) farther north to allow the advance to continue. John Wood's tanks were reinforced with a regiment from the 35th Infantry for the advance, and they made rapid progress towards Sens on the evening of 21 August, to find surprised German officers parading through the town centre in their dress uniforms. The division also secured a crossing of the River Yonne, as well as capturing five railway trains comprising

50 wagons of diesel oil and 305 tonnes (300 tons) of food. The 35th Division's official history described the aftermath:

"At Sens the Yanks were enthusiastically welcomed by the delighted French, and, as in Orléans, there were numerous parades, demonstrations and public gatherings. Caught unaware, the Nazis had no time to remove the huge piles of supplies they had gathered. Warehouses and storage caves yielded large stores of canned goods, flour, chocolate, and other foodstuffs. For many days afterward, Yanks had hotcakes for breakfast made from German buckwheat. There were also many enemy vehicles in good repair and a number of prisoners were captured."

When Eddy telephoned Patton to report his success at taking Sens, the shocked corps commander was told to "hang up [the phone] and keep going".

■ *Above:* Two concealed US GIs prepare to fire their Bazooka anti-tank rocket at a German halftrack near Andaine, France.

■ *Above:* **Diving for cover, a US trooper in action. Though Patton is famous for his armoured exploits, much of what he achieved could not have happened without the average infantry private.**

The 4th Armored Division rolled on towards Troyes on the Seine, where several hundred Germans were reportedly holed up.

Meanwhile the 134th and the 320th Infantry Regiments of the 35th Infantry Division secured crossings over the River Yonne to open the road to Troyes. On 21 August the 320th occupied the town of Pithiviers and the high ground in that vicinity without opposition, while the 134th began a movement to the east. The regiments were in combat team formation, linking infantry and artillery under a single command.

On 22 August, Combat Team 134 moved into position to attack Montargis and only scattered resistance was encountered, including roadblocks and ambushes by armoured vehicles. By noon on 23 August, one battalion was advancing in an encircling movement around the southern edge of the town. Combat Team 320, in the meantime, took positions on the high ground west of the town after fighting through light opposition to the northeast. By nightfall Montargis was in the hands of Combat Teams 134 and 320.

The next day Combat Team 320 moved by foot to take Courtenay and conducted mopping-up operations while *en route*. Combat Team 134 also advance several miles east on 25 August by truck to seize and hold the town of Joigny. Both combat teams then mopped up for several days. Combat Team 134 alone captured over 900 prisoners on 26 August. The 134th Infantry Regiment's official history recounted the demoralized state of German troops more than two months on from D-Day:

"Now the French brought a report that there were a hundred or more Nazis near Villemer who were willing to surrender; but they would surrender only to Americans. Here was a task cut out for the regimental intelligence officer, Major Dale M. Godwin. With a reinforced platoon from the 3rd Battalion's Company I and Sergeant Bloch, the interpreter, the S-2 moved out in quest of prisoners. After a couple of changes in direction, the column approached the town where the enemy was reported to be. Stopping the trucks above the military crest of a small hill, where they would be safe from direct fire, the major and interpreter dismounted, took a white flag, and walked down the dusty road toward the enemy position. On arrival, they found a typical 'Hollywood' Nazi in command. Asked to surrender, he replied that he

would like four hours to think it over. Major Godwin told him to come out within 30 minutes, or all the artillery at his disposal (which was very little) would be brought down. Officers with the small task force made every effort they could to get some artillery fire within that time, but had little success. Fortunately, some artillery from somewhere did fall in the general vicinity. After some delay, a group of about 50 Germans came over the hill to surrender. Shortly after, another group of 26 came up the road on bicycles. Soon a two-and-a-half-ton truck was in regular shuttle service hauling prisoners. This particular source of prisoners ceased only when, late in the afternoon, the 3rd Battalion was ordered to move on to St. Florentin, [26

■ *Below:* Troops of the US 35th Infantry Division in action against enemy forces west of Paris in August 1944.

■ *Right:* US soldier
Private Raymond
Ruark guards a
roadblock near
Domfront with his
.30in-calibre
machine gun.

■ *Left:* General Patton (far right) takes a trip to visit his armoured formations at the front. He liked nothing more than being in the field, commanding his army.

kilometers] 17 miles) farther east. But prisoners were coming from other units of the Regiment.

"One of the more spectacular of the actions in this multi-ring circus of gathering up Germans was that of the Anti-tank Company. This action, as all such should be, was the result of active reconnaissance and the exercise of initiative and aggressive leadership. First-Lieutenant William P. Sheehy of Nebraska, an anti-tank platoon leader on motor reconnaissance over the roads in the Joigny vicinity, noticed groups of Germans in a field some distance away. Sheehy's immediate reaction was to open fire, though it might have meant a hostile and dangerous response from the more numerous enemy. The Germans retired to a wood, however, and when Sheehy led a patrol down to the woods, he returned with 42 prisoners. Anti-tank guns opened fire on a German

column on the road, and the lieutenant directed additional fire into the woods. Results were decisive in a space of time hardly to be reckoned in minutes. Destroyed material cluttered the road, there were all kinds of motor vehicles and numbers of horses to be had, and the Anti-tank Company contributed more than 300 prisoners to the regimental cages. By the end of the day, no less than 796 German soldiers had been retired from the opposition by the prisoner-of-war route."

Throughout XII Corps' advance XIX Tactical Air Command's fighters patrolled ahead of its columns to neutralize any German resistance and prevent the Luftwaffe interfering with the US advance. The 4th Armored was attacked on 23 August near Sens, forcing US fighter-bombers to break off an air-strike mission to protect Wood's men. On another occasion Otto

■ Above: A German Tiger tank destroyed by a P-51 Mustang. These heavy weapons were fearsome and almost invulnerable to any US tank round. Fortunately for Patton, Weyland's pilots were always on hand to take on German heavy tanks.

Weyland's pilots intercepted and broke up an attack by 70-plus German Focke-Wulf Fw-90 fighter-bombers before they could get through to their targets. On 25 August, the Allies launched a major air strike to knock out in a single blow the remaining Luftwaffe airfields in France that had been pinpointed by Ultra. These attacks were particularly successful and neutralized the threat to Patton's troops as they entered the final phase of their campaign in France. Overall, USAAF aircraft destroyed some 254 aircraft in the campaign, with Weyland's men claiming 67 kills. The interdiction effort against retreating German columns continued unabated, with 164 railway carriages, 44 locomotives, 266 motor vehicles and 4 tanks claimed destroyed by Weyland's fighters on 25 August alone.

Corporal Albert Maranda of the 4th Armored Division's 94th Armored Field-Artillery Battalion recounted in his diary the subsequent confused and chaotic advance to Troyes.

"*21 August:* Rained early this morning. Can't complain, have had very good weather since landing in France. Moved out at 08:35 hours. Took secondary roads most of the way. Bypassed Orléans by [5 kilometers] 3 miles. Raining quite hard, getting soaked. Went through Sens, quite a large and beautiful city. People crowded up so bad it was hard to get through. Bivouacked [8 kilometers] 5 miles outside Sens.

"*22 August:* Gassed up – cleaned up guns etc. A bit of artillery fire. Germans on three sides of us. We are the furthest advanced outfit to the east there is. Everybody is quite surprised at the small amount of Germans in this area. Sens is quite a rail center. Have taken about 150 prisoners in all. Germans have moved out of range of our guns.

"*23 August:* Got up quite late – ate – wrote letter to Ma. Laid around. Played cards, won 300 Francs. 15 German planes came over, we fired on them. Rumor has it 13 were shot down and one [US] P-47 shot down. 24 E [squad] picked up one German pilot, he was badly burnt. Men in HQ Battery picked up German sniper, he was 18 years old. Got letters of 30 July and 3 August from Ma.

"*24 August:* Laid in bed, not much doing. Played cards, won about 100 Francs. Had fresh meat for dinner and supper. Test-fired a carbine. A little activity from Jerry. Paris captured by Free French of the Interior (FFI) with the help of the Americans who surrounded the city. We are pulling out tomorrow, headed for Troyes."

Wood had just received orders to continue the march eastwards and capture Troyes and the key bridges in the town. Combat Command A, under Colonel Bruce Clarke, was to take the town while Combat Command B outflanked the objective from the south.

Objective Troyes

Clarke's troops moved out from Sens on the morning of 25 August in two columns, with a battalion-sized task force of armoured vehicles, commanded by Major Arthur L. West, leading the way. In the middle of the afternoon West's tanks and halftracks reached the outskirts of Troyes and halted on a ridge to send scouts forward to check out intelligence reports that only a few hundred rear echelon troops were based there, dismantling supply dumps in preparation to withdraw eastwards.

As the afternoon progressed, West's men were coming under increasingly heavy and accurate artillery fire, so the major decided to put his attack plan into action. Using so-called desert tactics, he formed his troops into a single line with tanks and halftracks intermingled and ordered them to charge straight into the town. The risks were high, as armoured vehicles can suffer high losses if they became bogged down in urban fighting

No easy victory

At top speed the US troopers raced towards the town, dodging artillery shells, a railway line and an anti-tank ditch. West ordered his men to press on, regardless of the loss of two tanks to German shells. GIs debussed from halftracks at the anti-tank ditch to mop up German artillery observers and ran into determined resistance. It later emerged that a full brigade of Waffen-SS troops were garrisoning the town, and they had little inclination to give it up.

Once the attack reached the town's outskirts, West ordered his men to split into two groups to press on and take the town square and the key bridges. Speeding through the narrow streets, the US troops took the Germans by surprise within a few minutes and seized their initial objectives. They then sent out patrols to link up with the French Resistance and take full control of the town's key buildings and facilities. A local baker briefed the GIs on the German positions and it dawned on West and his officers that they might had bitten off more than they could chew. Now the Germans recovered their composure and started to launch counter-attacks. By the time it was getting dark, the Americans were penned into two small perimeters. Sniping and ambushes continued throughout the night as both sides probed for weaknesses in their opponents' positions.

Clarke established radio contact with West inside Troyes, who told him to hold tight until the morning, when he hoped to push a rescue column through to him and his beleaguered men.

Four combined tank-infantry companies were organized for the relief mission to attack from multiple

■ *Above:* **Three batteries of a Third Army Field Artillery battalion open fire in late August 1944. They are using M102 105mm howitzers, which had a range of over 15km (10 miles).**

directions to confuse the Germans and allow West's men to attack outwards to link up with the relief force. The attacks went in at dawn, surprising and overrunning the German artillery battery and its main command post, and killing an SS general in the process. The assault force then rolled forward to link up with West in the two squares. The reinforced US contingent now spread out to attack several German strongholds in the town, including the headquarters of the feared secret police, the Gestapo. American tanks blasted the building, leaving 58 dead Germans inside while another 50 came out with their hands up.

Another armoured infantry battalion arrived just before midday to take over the job of mopping up the last pockets of German resistance. By the time they had finished, more than 1100 Germans were either dead or captured. German material losses included 53 vehicles, 10 artillery pieces, 53 anti-tank guns, 72 machine guns and thousands of small arms. US losses were 3 vehicles destroyed, 15 killed and 55 wounded. With Troyes and its key bridges clear, Wood's armour now had an open road to the east.

To XII Corps' left, Walker's XX Corps was also moving quickly to reach its objectives. The 5th Infantry Division moving by truck reached Fontainebleau on 20 August, only to find the Germans had blown the bridge over the Seine. Assault boats were brought up and a

157

bridgehead secured after an assault river crossing succeeded in driving away the German defenders. Other XX Corps troops also managed to ford the Seine at Montereau with the help of the French Resistance. The 5th Infantry then pushed forward to protect the flank of XII Corps, with its 2nd Infantry Regiment getting involved in a stiff fight with several thousand German troops at Bauillet on 21 August. The division took Romilly on 25 August.

The 7th Armored in action

The 7th Armored Division was given Melun, 32km (20 miles) south of Paris, as its objective and this was to prove a far tougher nut to crack. Delays in getting XX corps started meant Ultra intelligence reports that its objective was weakly held were out of date by the time the division arrived at the Seine. Lindsay Silvester hoped to seize the town's main bridge in a surprise attack, but the 7th Armored's spearhead ran into fierce resistance and took heavy losses from well-placed machine guns and artillery. Despite heavy US artillery support and several air strikes, the Germans could not be budged and managed to blow the key bridge up in the full view of the American troops.

The 7th Armored Division's Combat Command A had been sent north of the town to seize another bridge over the Seine in the hope of outflanking Melun. It also ran into heavy resistance and could not stop the bridge being blown up. Infantrymen were then pushed over the river in assault boats and they secured a toehold, enabling engineers to begin building a pontoon bridge during the night. Walker now arrived at the riverbank opposite Melun and ordered an immediate assault across the ruins of the bridge, but heavy German fire brought the attack to a halt with severe losses.

The flanking attack was now gathering momentum and soon tanks

■ *Above left:* **General de Gaulle (second from left), Free French leader, stands next to General Leclerc after the recapture of Paris.**

■ *Left:* **General Dietrich von Choltitz (centre) surrenders Paris to the Allies.**

■ *Above:* **Jubilant scenes around the Arc de Triomphe in August 1944.**

were over the Seine, heading for Melun. Minefields delayed their advances for several hours, though, and it was not until the early hours of 25 August that they were able to break the back of the German defence in the town.

Patton's advance south of Paris had completely unhinged the German defence of Paris, which had now risen in revolt against its occupiers.

Realizing the city was undefendable, the German commander of Paris, Lieutenant-General Dietrich von Choltitz, ignored Hitler's orders to blow up historic buildings all over the city. He surrendered with his garrison on 25 August, Leclerc's armoured columns then entering the city to complete its liberation. Patton was denied the glory

of heading the US troops that followed in Leclerc's wake into Paris. His army was still fighting fiercely to the north and south of the French capital, engaging German forces retreating across the River Seine.

General Patton's use of Ultra intelligence, combined with airpower and rapid armoured strikes, had again proved a winning combination during the advance to the Seine. Melvin Helfers, Patton's Ultra intelligence officer, recalls being called over by the General at this time for a briefing information on the latest German deployments. "After it was all over with, he said, 'Thank you very much Major, you have just saved me the service of two divisions'."

CHAPTER 7

CLEARING THE WEST BANK

"The British were asked to do this but said they could not move fast enough. This was true."

Patton, 19 August 1944

As Patton's Third Army raced to the Seine, it left the German forces that had escaped from Falaise totally exposed. Allied intelligence estimated that some 75,000 Germans, with 25,000 vehicles and 250 tanks, were fleeing northwards to the Seine. In reality there was probably twice as many Germans west of the Seine, and they were desperate to escape the trap being set for them by Patton.

Not surprisingly, Patton was keen to swing his XV Corps northwards from Dreux to seize the crossings over the Seine north of Paris. After days of prevarication, Bradley allowed Patton to move his troops to the Seine at Mantes-Gassicourt, 32km (20 miles) north of the French capital.

Wade Haislip had barely stopped his XV Corps at Dreux when he received his new orders early on 18 August. The road was open and the 79th Division reached the Seine unopposed later that day. The division's route of advance had been carefully selected by Patton on advice from his Ultra intelligence liaison officers, who had used intercepted German communications to plot a line of march that avoided German

■ *Left:* German machine-gun fire opens up on a US ferry as it attempts a river crossing near Montereau, 50km (30 miles) southeast of Paris. Fortunately for these US troops the Germans did not have any mortars.

■ *Left:* At Mantes-Gassicourt, US combat engineers construct a ferry to cross the River Seine. Without the skills of these men, Patton's armour would not have been able to make their thrusting drives into France.

strongpoints. XIX Tactical Air Command's fighter-bombers were also unleashed on the German lines of communications over the Seine, with 20 river barges claimed destroyed and another 91 damaged on 19 August alone. Allied air superiority was having a telling effect.

Again Bradley was unsure what to do when presented with this prize by Patton. He was worried that by pushing northwards along the Seine Patton's troops would enter the zone of General Montgomery's British and Canadian armies, causing what was termed an "administrative headache" as the supply lines of three armies became hopelessly tangled together.

Bradley's mind was made up later on 18 August after a meeting with Montgomery, in which the British general declared: "This is no time to relax or to sit back and congratulate ourselves. Let's finish off the business in record time." Patton received new orders. XV Corps was to push down the west bank of the Seine and seize a

bridgehead over the river to allow an advance on Beauvais, to cut off German troops already heading eastwards.

Poor roads and difficult terrain on the west bank of the Seine made Patton favour putting more troops over the river. His views were overruled, but Patton was not going to be accused of slacking. Haislip was quickly ordered to push across the Seine with the 79th Infantry Division and Lunsford Oliver's 5th Armored Division was to advance along the river's west bank, while XIX Corps of Courtney Hodges' First Army came up on its left flank.

Patton arrived during 19 August to encourage the men of the 79th Infantry Division as they prepared for their coming offensive. Reconnaissance patrols found a small dam across the 244m (800ft) -wide river and in heavy rain the 313rd Infantry Regiment crossed to the east bank of the Seine late in the evening. Combat engineers then used assault boats to ferry the first parts of a pontoon bridge across the river. During 20 August another infantry regiment crossed the Seine in more assault boats to expand the bridgehead. By later in the day the bridge was complete and another infantry regiment crossed in trucks. Rocket-firing German bombers now appeared in an attempt to destroy the new bridge, but were driven off with the loss of a dozen aircraft to American anti-aircraft gunners. Over the next four days more than 50 German aircraft were claimed destroyed by Patton's gunners.

The 79th Infantry Division rapidly moved to push all its combat elements across the Seine, and they soon spread out to clear up pockets of German resistance, seize bridges and interrupt barge traffic. Headquarters personnel of the German Army Group B's command post at La Roche-Guyon had to make a quick escape to avoid being overrun by the 79th Infantry Division. Bradley, however, insisted that the main XV Corps axis of advance be south of the Seine, so the 79th Infantry was not able to exploit its success.

The 5th Armored turned north from Mantes and headed up the west bank of the Seine, only to run into heavy resistance from elements of eight German divisions, including several Waffen-SS units. They had been sent south to cover the withdrawal of three German armies heading for temporary ferries set up around Rouen. Ravines, rain, fog and numerous ambushes reduced the 5th Armored Division's advance to a snail's pace. It took the

■ *Below:* After initial elements had secured a foothold on the far side of the river, Third Army engineers could then construct pontoon bridges such as this one, to ferry more tanks and men across.

■ *Left:* A Luftwaffe Focke-Wulf Fw-190 fighter-bomber. Though the Allies had control of the skies, some German ground-attack aircraft managed to harass the Third Army.

■ *Below:* A PAK 43 88mm anti-tank gun. This dedicated anti-armour weapon was a variant of the same gun used in Tiger II and Jagdpanther tanks. It could easily knock out a Sherman tank.

■ *Right:* A
knocked-out Third
Army M4 Sherman
tank on the road to
the Seine. What
the Sherman
lacked in firepower
and armour
protection, it made
up for in reliability
and speed.

division five days to reach Elbeuf near the entrance to a loop in the River Seine, upstream from Rouen.

It took the 5th Armored 10 hours to reach the Seine south of Bonnières during the afternoon of 18 August. In this race it overran several groups of enemy infantry and destroyed one 150mm howitzer, two halftracks and numerous trucks.

Lunsford Oliver then pivoted his division to face north and started to push up the west bank of the Seine. He advanced two combat commands abreast, with the town of Vernon as his division's first objective. At first his units ran into disorganized and dispirited Germans, who were surrendering in the hundreds. More fanatical Waffen-SS soon began to enter the fight, however, turning XV Corps' advance into a bloody, close-quarter dogfight.

In this confused situation, German and American columns soon became intermingled. The 5th Armored's 81st Tank Battalion was in the process of

rounding up a large group of German prisoners when the outfit's commanding officer spotted a convoy of what appeared to be ambulances making for the Seine. When the German vehicles drew level with the American tanks, the occupants opened fire with submachine guns. The GIs returned fire, raking the German vehicles and forcing five Waffen-SS men to surrender. Later that evening, the US tank crews bivouacked for the night when they heard the sound of strange tracked vehicles approaching. After firing flares to illuminate what turned out to be a German Panther, the Sherman crews raced to their tanks and began firing on the enemy vehicle. Their 75mm shells just bounced off the Panther's armour until it was 5m (16.4ft) away from one Sherman, when a lucky round ricocheted off the side of its turret and penetrated the engine compartment. This set the German tank on fire, and its crew abandoned the vehicle.

Similar scenes were repeated on 19 August as the 5th Armored's advance gathered momentum. Isolated German anti-tank guns posted at crossroads attempted to hold up the American advance, and company sized groups of German infantry were encountered. More than 30 German fighter-bombers also tried to strafe the American columns. In the evening the first resistance from German panzers was encountered as the 5th Armored occupied high ground along the Seine. From here, Oliver's troopers could see the Eiffel Tower in downtown Paris, way to the south. They, however, were to be denied the pleasurable duty of liberating the French capital.

On 20 August, the division was ordered to press on 40km (25 miles) to the north, to cut off the escape of German units heading to cross the Seine

at Les Andelys, where several pontoon bridges and ferries were shuttling 27,000 German troops to safety.

German resistance was fierce and determined at this point, and Combat Command A soon ran into 12 to 15 German tanks entrenched in excellent defensive positions, which allowed their guns to sweep all approaches to the south of the town. For three hours during the afternoon US fighter-bombers, artillery and tank destroyers brought down fire on the German tanks, but only a few of the Panthers yielded any ground. By the end of the day, the Germans had lost 12 tanks, destroyed by both ground and air action, for the loss of 3 Shermans and 3 tank destroyers. Lieutenant-Colonel Hernandez of the 628th Tank Destroyer

■ *Below:* Two US soldiers, armed with a Bazooka anti-tank rocket launcher, wait for the German halftrack in the distance to move into range.

■ Right: The fearsome Panther tank, minus one track. As a British soldier remarked upon seeing one for the first time, "the weight of its armour and the length of its gun were not heartening". These thoughts were no doubt echoed by the men of Patton's army.

Battalion was killed while directing fire in front of his own guns. Elements of the 7th Armored were sent to reinforce 5th Armored's attack during the day when it appeared to be stalling.

Heavy fighting raged throughout 21 August in the woods and small villages along the banks of the Seine, as more German tanks and infantry were fed into the battle.

The attacks resumed on 22 August. It was reported that two enemy Panther tanks had infiltrated into Combat Command A's position during the night, and had knocked out three light tanks just after daylight. Fortunately for the Americans the infiltrating tanks were destroyed. The fog was so dense at this point that observation for artillery fire was impossible, giving the Germans an advantage. Fighting escalated sharply throughout the day, as a tank-heavy battlegroup of the Waffen-SS 12th *Hitlerjugend* Panzer Division was thrown into the battle to stop the American advance, which was aimed to outflank the town of Vernon.

When US troops tried to advance across flat, open ground to the north of the village of Champenard, they entered the field of fire of five Panthers and one towed 88mm flak gun, which were camouflaged in woods about 1097m (3600ft) to the northeast. These concealed enemy guns opened up a deadly fire, destroying two US tanks, three halftracks and three light tanks.

To clear the wooded fringes (around this open area on the north of Champenard) infantry dismounted from their halftracks and took their Bazookas into the woods with them. This pressure applied by the bazooka-firing infantrymen forced the German tanks to withdraw from the woods. But as they tried to escape to the north they came within view of US tanks, which immediately loosed a torrent of shells on them. Four of the Panthers were hit and the fifth was abandoned.

As the 5th Armored's lead task force was grinding forward northwest of Gaillon, it started receiving machine-gun fire from a harvested field. Under each heap of wheat was a large fox-hole in which SS troops lay waiting. As the GIs started to spread out in preparation for an attack on this fortified position, German anti-tank shells set two Shermans and two light tanks on fire. The attack threatened to stall, but US air and artillery liaison officers called for help, and soon the big shells were whining overhead and the fighter-bombers were diving on the enemy gun positions. At the same time, the GIs turned their tank, assault and machine guns on the woods hiding the German tanks. A tracer bullet from one of the weapons ignited a drum of gasoline mounted on one of the Panthers. This blazing marker enabled XIX Tactical Air Command easily to pick out and quickly destroy two more Panther tanks.

The Shermans then started to shoot up the wheat stooks and the unyielding Waffen-SS troops who were concealed in the fox-holes beneath them. US infantry then moved in, and with their grenades and rifles finished off those Germans who still resisted. During the fight not a single Waffen-SS man offered to surrender. When the Graves Registration personnel gathered up the crop of dead on this wheat field the next day, they counted the bodies of 200 German soldiers.

The following day, the 5th Armored's tank and infantry units continued to clear the woods north from Champenard, as artillery batteries and fighter-bombers were kept busy smashing up two Seine-bound German columns, which they caught on roads

■ *Below:* German prisoners taken by the Third Army are marched off to a POW camp by an American GI in late August 1944.

ahead of the division. These included an armoured force and a horse-drawn artillery column. US pilots were now expert at spotting enemy tank tracks and following them until they disappeared in haystacks, buildings and clumps of trees. These innocent-looking objects would then be hit by the airmen with their bombs and rockets.

During 24 August heavy rain turned the battlefield into a mud-bath and slowed the American advance to a snail's pace. German resistance was still tenacious, but the back of their resistance had been broken with the defeat of the Waffen-SS counterattack two days earlier. Late in the day, the 5th Armored Division secured Heude-bouville, thus cutting the German escape route to Les Andelys.

The spearhead units of the division were now ordered to halt and hand over the advance to elements of the First Army coming up on their left flank. Over the next two days, it pulled back to assembly areas behind the 79th Infantry Division at Mantes-Gassicourt, and from there it provided artillery support for US bridgeheads on the eastern bank of the Seine.

The 5th Armored Division was now transferred from Patton's Third Army to the First Army for the remainder of the campaign in northwest Europe. According to the division's official history, its almost month-long period in combat was of record length. In this long session of continuous fighting from Normandy to the Seine, the division left in its wake a clutter of broken enemy

units and destroyed equipment. The division killed 2811 German soldiers and captured a further 2900. It destroyed 203 tanks, 8 armored cars, 384 motor vehicles, 3 ambulances, 20 self-propelled guns, 87 artillery pieces, and 89 infantry weapons. And it captured 36 tanks, 8 aircraft and 18 artillery pieces.

In its campaign from Normandy to the Seine, the 5th Armored Division travelled a distance of 648km (405 miles). This figure is actually the shortest road distance, but many individual manoeuvring vehicles of the division recorded more than 960km (600 miles). The armoured drive included the move from St-Sauveur-le-Vicomte to south of the Selune River, 136km (85 miles); the advance to Le Mans, 152km (95 miles); the advance

north to Argentan, 93km (58 miles); the advance to Dreux, 128km (80 miles); the advance to the Seine, 56km (35 miles); and the advance to the northwest point of Eure-Seine Pocket and back again, 83km (52 miles).

British and Canadian troops were now hot on the heels of the Germans, and by 24 August only a German bridgehead behind Elbeuf was holding out west of the Seine. Allied artillery and airpower swept the narrow bridgehead relentlessly, inflicting heavy losses on the German convoys, which were forced to move in daylight to escape over the river ferries. A 50,000-strong German rearguard kept the Allied forces at bay until 25 August, when Hitler's commander in northern France, Field Marshal Walther Model, gave the order to pull back the rearguard

■ *Above Left:* **Field Marshal Walther Model, Hitler's commander in northern France. He was brought in to replace Kluge, and stabilized the front at the West Wall in September 1944.**

■ *Above:* A US M18 Hellcat tank destroyer of VIII Corps fires its 76mm gun point-blank at a German pillbox in Brest. This vehicle was generally used in "shoot and scoot" tactics and was very effective.

and establish a new defensive line along the River Seine.

It took until 27 August for the last troops of the Fifth Panzer Army to escape across the river. The experience so exhausted the survivors that any hopes of holding the Seine had been utterly dashed. What was left of the German Army in France was in headlong retreat for the border of the Third Reich. Hitler was issuing daily directives calling for new defensive lines to be set up, but this was pure fantasy. Though his troops made token efforts to hold up the Allies, German commanders in France considered these little more than tactical rearguard actions, to give them more time to escape with the bulk of their troops.

By the beginning of the last week in August, Patton's Third Army was stretched from Brittany to the far banks of the Seine south of Paris, where XX and XII Corps were poised for further advances to the east. Haislip's XV Corps had been temporarily detached to the First Army for the final stages of the battles south of Rouen, while Troy Middleton's VIII Corps was in the final stages of liquidating the German garrison of Brest. The 38,000-strong garrison finally surrendered on 18 September, after being bombarded for almost three weeks by a British battleship and most of XIX Tactical Air Command's strike aircraft. The port was in ruins. By this point the need for the 6th Armored Division in Brittany was over, and it was at this time rapidly driving eastwards to join up with the rest of Patton's armour for the next phase of the French campaign.

This left Patton with an exposed southern flank some 720km (450 miles) in length, and very few troops to guard it. The main worry for Patton was an attack by German troops retreating from southern France, where the US Seventh Army had landed in the middle of August and was rapidly moving north to link up with the Third Army.

Patton now took a calculated risk and relied on intelligence from the Ultra code-breaking operation to warn him of any threats to his flank. Rather than diverting scarce troops from his spearheads to holding his flanks, Patton gave the job to XIX Tactical Air Command and Otto Weyland. If Ultra warned him of a German threat, then airpower would have to deal with the problem.

Following the successful conclusion of the St-Malo–Dinard campaign in Brittany, the 83rd Infantry Division also moved to the Loire Valley to protect the entire right flank of the Third Army in its dash across France. The mission began on 22 August and concluded on 20 September. The zone of responsibility assigned to the division extended from the vicinity of St-Nazaire eastwards, along the Loire valley through Nantes, Angers, Tours and Orléans to Auxerre. This was a distance of more than 320km (200 miles) – the longest line of responsibility given to any division in the war. An 83rd Reconnaissance Troop patrol went south to Bordeaux without mishap. Another went south from Orléans and, near the Swiss border, contacted elements of General Patch's US Seventh Army moving north from the Mediterranean.

When a 36,000-strong German column started approaching the upper Loire valley from the south of France, Weyland's airmen sprung into action.

■ Above: A P-51D Mustang fighter-bomber. The aircraft of Weyland's XIX Tactical Air Command were instrumental in forcing the surrender of 20,000 Germans of General Elster's command on 7 September at the town of Beaugency.

■ *Above:* A destroyed German Tiger tank courtesy of XIX Tactical Air Command. The power of the explosion that knocked it out was so intense that it has been flipped onto its roof.

Every one of 18 railway and 16 road bridges on routes that linked France with Germany were systematically destroyed by US strike aircraft, forcing the column to swing northwards. Then Weyland's fighter-bombers started to work over the German LXIV Corps, destroying hundreds of vehicles on a daily basis. In a 10-day period the German force was reduced to the status of pedestrians, short of water and food. French Resistance fighters were also snapping at the heels of the Germans, giving them no respite.

The desperate German commander, Brigadier-General Botho Elster, sent an envoy to find the nearest American ground unit, with the plea, "Keep the *Jabo* (German slang for fighter-bomber, Jagdbomber) off my men and they will march north to Beaugency bridge, [48km] 30 miles southwest of Orléans." Weyland told the German to head for

Beaugency with white flags or face further air strikes. The nearest US ground unit was the 83rd Division, then assigned to General William Simpson's Ninth Army that was moving from Normandy to the front east of Paris, and it was sent to take the surrender of the surviving shell-shocked 20,000 men of Elster's command.

At the surrender ceremony on 7 September, when the 83rd Infantry Division's commander announced he was accepting the capitulation of Elster and his men, the German general pointedly turned his back on the American and marched over to Weyland. Elster then announced he was only going to surrender to the man who had forced his surrender – Patton's right-hand man in the sky, Brigadier-General Otto Weyland. This was the largest mass surrender to date of German troops in France.

CHAPTER 8

TO THE GERMAN BORDER

"We have at this time, the greatest chance to win the war ever presented. It is such a sure thing that I am sure these blind moles don't see it."

Patton, 21 August 1944.

The final week of August 1944 saw the Allied armies in France occupying Paris and several bridgeheads across the Seine on either side of the French capital. German troops were in headlong retreat. At this point in the campaign Eisenhower began to assert himself as Supreme Commander of the Allied Expeditionary Force, and soon set his mark on Allied strategy for the remainder of the campaign in Europe.

The British were keen for a push along the Channel coast to Belgium, to clear out the German V-weapon sites that were still causing thousands of casualties in London and southeast England. Montgomery proposed that his armies receive the bulk of the supplies flowing across the Normandy beaches to allow them to push on into the Netherlands, and then hook right into the Ruhr, the heartland of German war production. Patton and other American commanders were horrified at the idea of the British getting the opportunity to "win the war", and were lobbying hard for the bulk of the scarce supplies of

■ *Left:* Tank transporters form part of a "Red Ball Express" convoy as they rattle through a French town to support the advancing forces of the US Third Army.

fuel, food and ammunition to go to the US armies driving hard for the German border at Metz, and then on to the River Rhine itself.

US troops now outnumbered British and other Empire forces in France, so American commanders claimed that they should be given the lion's share of the glory of supplies to win the war. Eisenhower decided to compromise, and give neither set of rival commanders their wish. He opted for what he called a "Broad Front" strategy. British and US armies would receive equal shares of supplies, particularly fuel, and advance in line abreast across France to the German border. According to Eisenhower, this would keep the pressure on the Germans along the whole of the Western Front and prevent them regrouping to launch a flanking counterattack against an exposed Allied spearhead. As far as Patton was

concerned, this was nothing less that a "sell-out" to the British. The Third Army commander was regularly heard complaining that Ike had lost a golden opportunity to win the war in 1944.

In spite of Patton's bluster, the supply problems facing the Allied troops in France at this time were immense. The German campaign to hold or sabotage the English Channel and west-coast ports had denied the Allies access to a means to bring huge cargo ships into port for unloading. Everything the Allied armies needed, from tank shells to fuel and toothpaste, had to be brought ashore across the Normandy invasion beaches using the man-made Mulberry harbours.

The rapid advance to the Seine put the ability of the Allied logistics chain to deliver these supplies to frontline units under great strain. The Third Army was at the extreme limit of these supply

■ *Above:* **Third Army troops ford another river during the advance east to the German border at the end of August 1944.**

■ *Right:* Eisenhower's "Broad Front" strategy, whereby the army groups fanned out to attack the German forces.

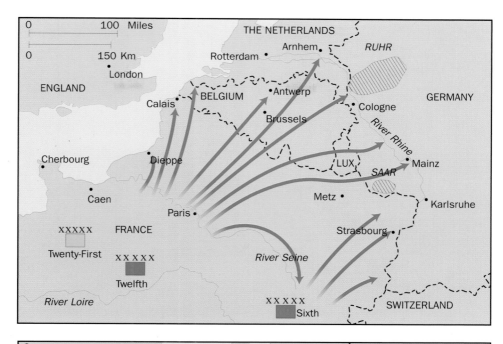

■ *Right:* The "Narrow Front" strategy. This was Montgomery's preferred plan, whereby the Allied army groups would stay largely together to punch into Germany.

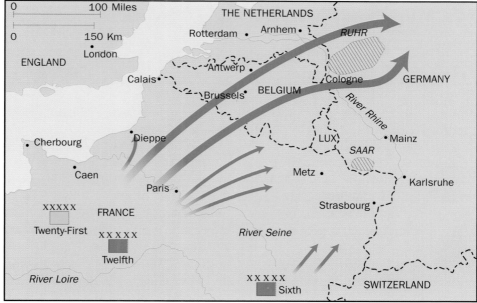

lines. Its equipment was worn from a month's continuous action, and its men were in urgent need of a rest. Even with his troops apparently stalled on the Seine, Patton was still generating ideas to push on to victory. On 23 August, he visited Bradley and proposed another "wide encirclement" move westwards to the Channel across the front of Montgomery's troops to trap the German columns retreating northwards from Rouen. Patton dubbed this the "best strategical [sic] idea I've ever had". Bradley tentatively approved the plan, and Patton set his staff to work making the necessary preparations.

While the fighting around Rouen on the lower Seine was reaching its climax, Eisenhower had finalized his plans for the "Broad Front" strategy, and details

of his orders began to filter down to subordinate commanders. The "wide envelopment" was cancelled.

Patton was given his orders on 24 August, and he was given a line of Metz-Strasbourg as his objective. Initially Patton was pleased to be advancing once again, and quickly set to preparing his men for action.

Emergency measures were put in train to resupply the Third Army in time for the new offensive. XIX Tactical Air Command opened its forward airfields south of Paris to accept aircraft bringing in fuel, rations, mail and other vital supplies. More than 250 C-47 Dakota transport aircraft of IX Troop Carrier Command flew into the recently captured Luftwaffe airfields on 25 August alone, and the effort peaked the following day when 606 Dakotas flew .977 million kilograms (2.15 million pounds) of fuel and rations to Patton's

troops. The so-called "Red Ball Express" system was instituted to speed supplies to the front. This involved 6000 trucks moving along dedicated one-way roads to and from the Normandy bridgehead. Patton also turned a blind eye to unofficial "foraging" by his supply chiefs, who went on "raids" to US First and Ninth Army depots to "liberate" fuel for the Third Army. Even with these measures, though, Patton's troops were desperately short of supplies. Indeed, only the capture of a huge German train with 37 wagons of fuel at Sens allowed XII Corps to refuel its tanks.

For the new offensive Patton was allocated seven divisions, under the control of XII and XX Corps. At this time XV Corps was still fighting north of Paris under First Army control, and VIII Corps was to be reassigned to the Ninth Army after it had completed its mission in Brittany.

■ *Above:* A convoy of 50 trucks of the "Red Ball Express" stops at a refuelling depot in France. Each truck could carry 6623 litres (1750 gallons) of fuel in jerrycans.

■ *Right:* Row upon row of jerrycans await transportation to the front. Patton's supply chiefs were not above "liberating" fuel from other American units for the Third Army's advance. All Allied armies were suffering from supply shortages during the autumn of 1944.

XX Corps' orders were to strike out northwards from its bridgeheads at Fontainebleau and Montereau to seize Reims, before swinging eastwards to advance level with XII Corps, which was to attack due east from Troyes towards the River Marne.

Patton struck out on 26 August in the face of minimal resistance. The 4th Armored Division led the XII Corps advance, motoring more than 80km (50 miles) to capture Vitry-le-François to cross the River Marne, knocking out four German 88mm flak guns posted to defend the town for no losses in the process. It then headed on to Châlons with the 80th Infantry Division close behind, before grinding to a halt when its tanks ran out of fuel. Scavenging secured more than 378,500 litres (100,000 gallons) of German petrol, allowing XII Corps to head towards Commercy on the River Meuse. The 4th Armored's rapid advance took the

■ *Above:* US troops of the Third Army use a captured German gun in France at the end of August 1944.

German defenders on the Meuse totally by surprise. Two detachments of Wood's division seized bridgeheads over the River Meuse on 31 August at St-Dizier, while the 80th Division took Commercy and St-Michel.

Otto Weyland's fighter-bomber squadrons joined the pursuit across eastern France, strafing German columns and adding hundreds more destroyed vehicles to their already impressive tally.

Intelligence reports now indicated that the enemy might attempt a counterattack, with the objective of recapturing Troyes and breaking through the southern flank of the Third Army. To prepare for this, the 35th Infantry Division mobilized Task Force "S" on 28 August, consisting of Combat Team 320, 737th Tank Battalion, and elements of the 654th Tank Destroyer Battalion. Its mission was to protect

Troyes from attacks from the east, southeast or south, and to clear the area north of the River Seine from the city to a line from Vendeuvre to Bar-sur-Seine. The force did this and then moved to the vicinity of Brienne-le-Château on 1 September. The remainder of the division continued its mission of flank protection until relieved by other XII Corps troops on 8 September.

Corporal Albert Maranda, of the 4th Armored Division's 94th Armored Field-Artillery Battalion, described the advance into Germany in his diary:

"*28 August:* Pulled out at 06:45 hours, headed for Vitry. Took secondary dirt roads. Reached Vitry at 11:15 hours. About 25 German planes came over but didn't bother us. Tanks and infantry had the city pretty well under control by 15:30 hours. Germans moving northeast fast. 'C' Battery stayed behind just in case. Rest of Battalion headed for Châlons – reached Châlons at 20:15 hours where rest of Combat Command

A has city under siege. Germans pretty well cut off, large fires started. We have crossed the Marne.

"*29 August:* Rained a bit. We are now in territory where last war was fought. Intermittent artillery fire. Germans are trying to escape but they are cut off. Tanks and Infantry moving up. Lieutenants Hoffman and Osborne say the Jerries were massacred. City in our hands after terrific artillery barrage at 13:05 hours. Tanks pushed what Germans escaped about [40 kilometers] 25 miles northeast. We head for St. Dizier tomorrow where Division & 3rd Army is supposed to assemble. Fired on German planes.

"*30 August:* Pulled out at 07:00 hours through Châlons to Vitry to St. Dizier. Part of Division already here just keeping the Germans from retreating. Tanks and Infantry moved in after the artillery laid down a barrage. Had the town pretty well cleaned up by 15:00 hours with the Germans on the run.

About 200 prisoners taken. Two German planes came over. Tomorrow we head for Commercy. Can't stop to assemble with 80th Division.

"31 August: Moved out at 09:10 hours. Followed main highway north through St. Dizier to Ligny where we took secondary roads to Commroy. Jerries putting up quite a fight. Passed through one town at 14:00 hours. A women told us the Jerries had been there just two hours previous, cleaning and shaving. They took off when they heard of our tanks.

"1 September: Germans shelled us intermittently during the night. Shells coming right over us and landing from one to a hundred yards away. About noon, about 25 German planes came over and bombed and fired rockets at us, no casualties.

"2 September: Tanks and Infantry inflicting heavy casualties on the Germans. About 300 prisoners taken. All of 80th moved in, but we can't move because we have outrun our gas and ammo supply points. Think the situation will be relieved tomorrow and we will move up to Nancy or directly to Metz. About [104 kilometers] 65 miles from German border now. Heard rumor that Nancy & Metz have been taken so that's that. Weather quite miserable, rainy and quite cool. Can't do much of anything except lay in bed under the tarp. Letter from Ma.

"3 September: Weather still miserable with only slight improvement – cleared up later in the day. Quite a few outfits have moved in around us. Managed to get to Ordnance & pick up some parts. Rode around Commercy, quite a nice town. Got there too late to witness the trials of some women that had doings with the Germans.

"4 September: Beautiful day today. Aired out my blankets – cleaned machine – wrote letter to Ma. News on

■ *Above:* Field Marshal Gerd von Rundstedt managed to galvanize the German defences in eastern France, and was also detailed to defend the Siegfried Line.

radio pretty good. Moving out tomorrow. Going up near Nancy."

In the XX Corps sector the 7th Armored Division led the way, advancing in six columns on a broad front to seize bridges over the River Marne south of Reims. The Germans managed to blow several bridges ahead of the 7th Armored, but it threw pontoon bridges across the obstacles blocking its way and was soon outflanking Reims to reach the River Aisne. Following up behind, the 5th Infantry's 11th Regiment was able to formally take the historic city of Reims on 30 August.

The 7th Armored then swung eastwards and headed towards Verdun. Driving through the Argonne Forest in heavy rain, the division joined up with French Resistance fighters to clear away

■ Above: Anti-tank "dragon's teeth" of the Siegfried Line. This extensive defensive network of tank traps and gun positions was designed to halt the Allied advance. However, it was far from impregnable.

the scattered German roadblocks that tried to hold up the advance. On the afternoon of 31 August, the 7th Armored was in Verdun and its tanks had taken control of a key bridge across the River Meuse. German air raids failed to destroy the bridge, and XX Corps was soon across in strength.

Patton was well positioned to strike for the River Moselle and the towns of Metz and Nancy. He hoped to strike fast and take them before the Germans had time to fortify them and block the route to the Siegfried Line or West Wall, a system of pillboxes and strongpoints built along the German western frontier in the 1930s and reinforced in the 1940s. However, frequent Ultra reports of new German reinforcements arriving opposite his troops on a daily basis made Patton very worried.

Now the supply lines to the Third Army finally ran dry, stranding Patton's tanks without fuel. The need to support the final attack on Brest also diverted much of XIX Tactical Air Command's aircraft away from the advance eastward. Patton had to wait for almost a week for extra fuel supplies to be brought forward before he could launch his troops forward again to seize a bridgehead over the Moselle. "Its not the Germans who have stopped us, but higher strategy," fumed Patton.

During that week the German defences on the Western Front solidified under the leadership of Field Marshal Gerd von Rundstedt, who had been called back to active service to command the defence of the Siegfried Line. The war in the West would not end in 1944.

CHAPTER 9

FIGHTING FOR LORRAINE

"God deliver us from our friends. We can handle the enemy."

Patton in Lorraine, September 1944

On 2 September 1944, Patton travelled to the headquarters of the US Twelfth Army Group for a conference of senior American military commanders in northwestern Europe. What he heard horrified the Third Army commander.

The precarious logistical situation of the Allied armies in France dominated the meeting. Eisenhower announced that he had decided to give Montgomery priority for fuel and ammunition over the coming weeks to allow him to clear up the Calais area and tidy up his supply lines. The idea of a knock-out blow into Germany by the Third Army before the winter was off the agenda. Patton would only be allowed to launch a "reconnaissance in force" to cross the River Moselle and launch a limited attack on the Siegfried Line. Even this limited action was only to be launched when fuel was available. A disillusioned Patton dubbed Eisenhower's decision "a fateful blunder".

He returned to his headquarters at La Chaume and resolved to exploit the limited opportunities open to him to

■ *Left:* Troops of the Third Army continue their assault across the River Meuse in September 1944. Though Patton's forces were unable to continue their thrust into Germany with such zeal, Patton made sure his men were constantly probing the line.

the maximum. His reconnaissance in force would be turned into a major offensive by stealth. "In order to attack we have to pretend to reconnoiter and then reinforce the reconnaissance and then finally attack," said Patton. "It is a very sad method of making war."

The normally cautious Bradley was equally outraged by Eisenhower's decision to back Montgomery, and he visited Patton on 3 September to offer the Third Army extra supplies from the First Army's allocation. Four extra divisions would also be made available to support Patton's offensive, but they would not be available until the middle of September. The Third Army would attack on 5 September.

Patton's initial offensive would aim to capture the two main cities of Lorraine, involving XX Corps, which was to seize the fortress of Metz, and XII Corps, which had Nancy as its objective.

His final objective was the River Rhine. Lorraine was perfect defensive terrain. Its many rivers and rolling wooded hills provided natural defence lines, and meant any attacker needed to prepare his assault carefully.

While Patton's troops had been halted by the shortage of fuel, the Germans had been building up their defences along the Moselle. Hitler, however, had bigger ambitions for his forces that were building up in Lorraine. He wanted them to launch a counter-attack into the southern flank of the US Third Army and then roll up the American line. Army Group G, under Colonel-General Johannes Blaskowitz, was assigned three panzer and panzer-grenadier divisions, as well as four independent panzer brigades, for the offensive. This force mustered some 600 tanks, mostly Panthers fresh from factories in Germany. The human

■ *Below:* General Patton visits one of his units at the front. He was determined to punch a hole right into Germany, despite all the difficulties he faced.

■ *Right:* The strategic situation in France on 1 September 1944. The Allies had pushed on to the border with the Low Countries, and the US Seventh Army was driving up from the south.

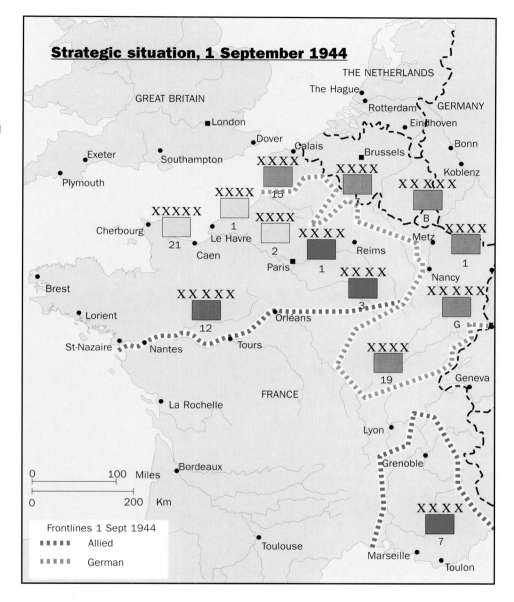

Strategic situation, 1 September 1944

resources available, however, left a lot to be desired. Most of the troops sent to the front were barely trained, and the new panzer brigades had had little time to train to anything like the level required to go into action. Blaskowitz, considered one of the Third Reich's leading tank generals, and his senior generals considered Hitler's plan to be fantasy. Their views cut little ice with the Führer, though, who wanted his offensive, come what may. Hitler was not interested in excuses. The scene was thus set for the biggest tank battles the Third Army had faced during its advance across France.

The drip-feeding of supplies to the Third Army meant Patton could only push his troops into battle when ammunition and fuel became available. There would therefore be no Third Army lightning offensive. In line with Eisenhower's "reconnaissance in force" policy, Patton planned a steadily escalating series of attacks to probe the German defences.

First into action was Horace McBride's 80th Infantry Division, which was ordered to seize a bridgehead across the River Moselle 16km (10 miles) south of Metz at Pont-à-Mousson on 5 September. The 3rd Panzergrenadier Division was waiting for the GIs, though, and inflicted 300 casualties before driving them back across the Moselle. This was a bad omen.

On the northern wing of the Third Army, XX Corps opened its attack on the same day with scouting probes towards Metz, prior to a full-scale offensive by the 7th Armored Division northeastwards towards the city up the west bank of the Moselle. This attack kicked off on 7 September, and the following day the 5th Infantry Division struck towards the Moselle at Dornot. German resistance was dogged and progress was very slow.

Night fight

With most of XX Corps' armour committed south of Metz, the Germans now decided to launch a spoiling attack north of the city to draw American forces away from their main thrust. The 106th Panzer Brigade was to spearhead this attack, with some 36 Panthers, 11 Jagdpanzer IV/70 self-propelled guns and 119 armoured halftracks. Their crews were green, and most had only been in the Wehrmacht for a few weeks.

The brigade was launched forward during the evening of 8 September in the hope of surprising the US 90th Infantry Division. During the night two German columns managed to dodge past American outposts and push deep behind American lines, coming to within a few metres of the 90th Division's command post. An alert sentry eventually spotted the attackers and a US Sherman opened fire, destroying a German halftrack. A confused battle now ensued in the woods surrounding the divisional

command post, with Shermans and Panthers trading fire in the darkness. Chaos reigned in the German force until daylight, when it renewed its attack southwards. By now, though, the American defence was gaining its cohesion. A US infantry battalion, backed by heavy artillery, halted the German brigade's main thrust in two hours of intense fighting. More than 300 rounds of 155mm fire knocked out seven Panthers and 20 halftracks. US tanks and an infantry battalion were

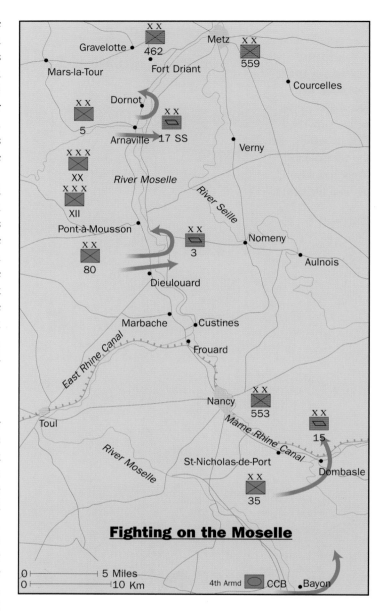

Fighting on the Moselle

■ *Above:* **The Third Army's attempts to cross the Moselle River. These crossings met with fierce resistance, and Patton's men were unable to gain much of a foothold.**

■ *Above:* Infantry of the Third Army hitch a lift on an M4 Sherman tank-dozer as it crosses the Moselle River.

now sent to trap the German escape route, catching them around the village of Mairy. The second German column was also halted by US anti-tank guns, which prevented it moving to relieve its cut-off comrades.

The battle raged for the remainder of the day, as the US troops moved in to mop up the remnants of the 106th Brigade. Some 21 Panthers and tank destroyers, 60 halftracks and 100 support vehicles were destroyed. Almost 800 Germans surrendered. The 106th Brigade effectively ceased to exist as a fighting force.

South of Metz, fighting raged as troops of the Waffen-SS 17th Panzergrenadier Division counterattacked against the 5th Division's bridgehead over the Moselle at Dornot, held by the 11th Infantry Regiment. The latter initially made a short advance, but were then subjected to 26 enemy counterattacks. Casualties were heavy and the regiment was forced to withdraw after three days of fighting. Next, the 10th Infantry Regiment attempted an assault, at Arnaville, south of where the 11th Regiment had been repelled. With two battalions of the 11th Regiment in support, the 10th Regiment pierced the German line and established a bridgehead. For the next five days the division beat off numerous German attacks in some of the fiercest fighting it experienced in the war. The 5th Division lost over 1400 men killed or wounded during the fighting south of Metz.

Patton hoped to push the 7th Armored through the Arnaville bridgehead to try to launch an encircling attack against Metz. Heavy German artillery sank a ferry carrying US reinforcements across the river, and then demolished a pontoon bridge, making it impossible to push any tanks across to support the infantrymen on the east bank. Heavy rain now descended on the battlefield, making it almost impossible to move supplies up to frontline areas. The attack on Metz had stalled.

The attack on Nancy

Farther south, Manton Eddy's XII Corps launched its own attack to take Nancy on 10 September. The 35th Infantry Division planned an assault river-crossing when scouts of its 134th Infantry Regiment's 2nd Battalion found an undamaged bridge at Flavigny that appeared undefended. By early evening the battalion was across the river. However, the Germans managed to destroy the bridge with artillery fire, and then the 15th Panzergrenadier Division counterattacked, wiping out the American battalion on 11 September, as recounted by the 134th Infantry Regiment's official history.

"At first everything went well for the 2nd Battalion after it started moving at 22:00 hours. Within an hour Companies E and F, a part of G Company, and a heavy machine-gun platoon had raced across the bridge. Then, as it appeared that success was imminent, the Nazi defenders discovered what was happening, and heavy artillery concentrations began to fall on us. Tank destroyers were ordered to the scene; one platoon was directed to cross immediately. But they failed to arrive in time; and the Germans were counterattacking with tanks.

"Then, at 01:30 hours, came a thunderous explosion on the bridge. An artillery shell – or, more probably, a sympathetic detonation of a fixed charge – had destroyed one of the spans. This left the men who had crossed in the extremely perilous position of facing an overwhelming counterattack with means neither for reinforcement nor for escape.

"Those men of the 2nd Battalion knew almost automatically that the thunderous explosion, ringing in their ears above all the fire that continued, signalled what they had dreaded most. They were cut off. Germans, screaming 'Heil Hitler!' closed in. Now, in the dark confusion which set in upon the lack of communication, the lack of contact, the lack of visibility, and the presence of Germans – with tanks – in their midst, individuals and small groups were on their own. For some, the prospect of facing German tanks without anti-tank defences – and of defending themselves when the only thing clear in the whole situation was that help could not reach them – all this was too overwhelming to be endured. Some counted on the blindness of the tanks at night, and reasoned that the darkness was as much a handicap to the Germans as to themselves. Others entered into no calculations whatever, they simply were seized with a determination never to give up.

"His instinct was to fight"

"One man of such determination was Sergeant Raymond M. Parker of Vermont. An assistant squad leader, Parker, cut off from his own unit, found himself with some machine gunners who were separated from their leaders. His instinct was to fight with whatever means might be at hand, and he lost no time in organizing a pair of makeshift machine-gun squads and getting the guns into action. But machine guns invite fire and death as well as dispense it, and enemy reaction soon exacted its toll; but then Parker himself manned one of the guns until his ammunition was exhausted. His means for defence eliminated, Parker soon fell into the hands of the Germans. It was only a temporary captivity, however, for the sturdy sergeant saw a fleeting opportunity and dived into the inky darkness

■ *Above:* US soldiers from Patton's Third Army cross the Moselle River. By the end of September 1944, the Allies were driving on towards Germany itself.

and ran toward the river. His first major obstacle was the Canal de l'Est, which ran in a concrete bed just along the northeast bank of the river. There was no time for hesitation, and he plunged into the water, reached the opposite side with a few quick strokes, and scrambled up the concrete bank. Without pause, he made for the river itself, and after a long swim – with a river current now to be fought – he made good his escape."

Farther up river, the 35th Division's 137th Infantry Regiment was thrown into the attack and secured several toeholds on the eastern bank. The GIs held long enough for Shermans of the 4th Armored Division's Combat Command B to cross the river and link up with them late on the night of 11 September. This was just in time, because early the following morning a battalion of Panthers was launched

against them. The presence of the American tanks saved the day and the attacking panzers were driven off with heavy losses. The Germans were using up their precious Panthers. The 4th Armored's assault was recounted by Eddy: "There was the cold, swift-running Moselle River with the Wehrmacht waiting in its 'winter line' on the east bank. With two tremendous blows, the 4th smashed across it in mid-September of 1944. Mediums of the 8th Tank Battalion rumbled into the Moselle Valley at Bayon, south of Nancy, on 11 September. The bridges were gone as well as the canal

parallelling it on the west. First-Lieutenant William C. Marshall didn't wait for treadway spans. He wheeled his medium tank platoon to the canal's edge, fired 75mm guns into the opposite bank to break it down, then threw logs into the mud and trickle. Gunning his tank, Lieutenant Marshall roared down the 20-foot canal and laboured triumphantly through to the other bank. He towed others of his platoon when they got bogged down. Five tanks raced downstream until the river split into three fordable channels. Water surged to the turrets as tanks plunged across the river. Climbing the

■ Above: At Nancy, an M4 Sherman of the 4th Armored Division fires upon a farmhouse containing German troops.

bank, tankers roared ahead to smash German infantry and guns pressing back the thin bridgehead."

Over the next two days, XII Corps managed to expand the southern bridgehead, but German resistance soon brought the advance to a halt.

Eddy had already turned his attention to strike at the north of Nancy, with the 80th Infantry Division pushing two battalions across the River Moselle on 11 September. For two days they managed to expand their bridgehead until a night-time counterattack by the 3rd Panzergrenadier Division, backed by 10 StuG III assault guns

(towards the end of the war StuGs were often issued to units as replacement for tank destroyers and even tanks), drove then back to within 100m (328ft) of the river bank. A company of Sherman tanks at last was brought up and, just at the last minute, managed to stabilize the situation. Before the German attack had been launched, Eddy and John Wood, commander of the 4th Armored, had already decided to commit the division's Combat Command A to the bridgehead. This force crossed into the bridgehead at the height of the battle and immediately started to trade fire with hull-down StuG IIIs. Eddy and

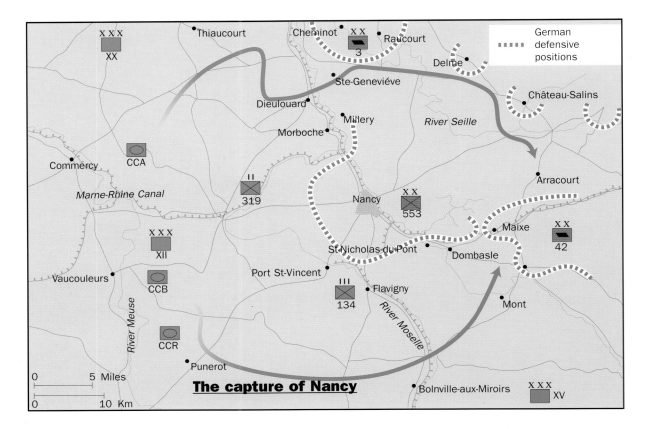

German defensive positions ·····

Thiaucourt · Cheminot · X X · Raucourt

X X X / XX

3

Delme ·

Ste-Geneviéve ·

Château-Salins ·

Dieulouard ·

Millery ·

Morboche · · *River Seille*

Commercy ·

CCA / ○

Marne-Rhine Canal

II / 319

Nancy · X X / 553

Arracourt ·

X X X / XII

St-Nicholas-du-Pont

Maixe · X X / 42

Dombasle ·

Vaucouleurs · CCB / ○

Port St-Vincent ·

III / 134 · Flavigny

Mont ·

River Meuse

CCR / ○

0 — 5 Miles

Punerot ·

The capture of Nancy

River Moselle

Bolnville-aux-Miroirs · X X X / XV

0 — 10 Km

Wood were watching the battle unfold from the west bank, and the German counterattack made them worry if it was wise to commit Colonel Bruce Clarke's tanks across a single bridge that was vulnerable to German artillery fire. In spite of not being able to deploy his full force of tanks in the narrow bridgehead, Clarke, the Combat Command A's leader, advised pressing ahead regardless, commenting, "Well, I can't fight the Germans on this side of the river." The 37th Tank Battalion, commanded by 30-year-old Lieutenant-Colonel Creighton Abrams, charged over the bridge and into the battle, battering its way past the Germans. Once through the frontlines, Abrams' Shermans ran amok among the confused German rear-echelon troops, reaching Château-Salins, 16km (10 miles) across the Moselle. During this advance the battalion destroyed 12 German armoured vehicles, 85 trucks and several

artillery pieces. From their new position, Clarke and Abrams were astride the supply route for the German garrison in Nancy, as the 35th Division, led by 4th Armored tanks, pushed up from the south threatening to close the ring. The XII Corps commander was full of praise for Wood's tank crews:

"4th Armored was loose again. Two steel columns tore into Lorraine to form pincers about Nancy. The city fell as the Germans fled east. Clarke's tanks punched through and rampaged behind enemy lines to Aulnois, Lemoncourt, Fresnes, Arracourt and Einville. More than 100 German tanks were destroyed, 1903 prisoners taken, as many killed. Rear echelon of a Panzergrenadier division was caught at Arracourt and wiped out. Combat Command B, south jaw of the pincers, gouged northeast to Château-Salins over streams and canals. The 24th Engineers, supported by the 995th Engineer Treadway Bridge

■ **Above: The movement of the Third Army as it attempted to encircle Nancy. The Germans were forced to evacuate the city after failing to push back the US tanks.**

Company, floated a 168-foot bridge over the Moselle at Bayon and a 180-foot bridge over the Meurthe at Mont. Halted by command once more to permit infantry to catch up, the 4th Armored stopped in the Arracourt area to protect the Nancy bridgehead."

This advance was no walkover, though, as the units met with strong German resistance. Sergeant Joseph Sadowski of the 37th Tank Battalion was posthumously awarded the Congressional Medal of Honor, the USA's highest decoration for valour,

■ *Right:* In the centre is General Hasso von Manteuffel. After the disaster at Nancy, Hitler gave him the daunting task of blunting Patton's attacks.

■ *Below:* Lieutenant-Generals Patton (left) and Bradley. Bradley's efforts were crucial to the Allied victory in France.

during an bloody engagement at Valhay. His citation commented, "On the afternoon of 14 September 1944, Sgt. Sadowski as a tank commander was advancing with the leading elements of Combat Command A, 4th Armored Division, through an intensely severe barrage of enemy fire from the streets and buildings of the town of Valhey. As Sgt. Sadowski's tank advanced through the hail of fire, it was struck by a shell from an 88mm gun fired at a range of 20 yards. The tank was disabled and burst into flames. The suddenness of the enemy attack caused confusion and hesitation among the crews of the remaining tanks of our forces. Sadowski immediately ordered his crew to dismount and take cover in the adjoining buildings. After his crew had dismounted, Sadowski discovered that one member of the crew, the bow gunner, had been unable to leave the tank. Although the tank was being subjected to a withering hail of enemy small-arms, bazooka, grenade, and mortar fire from the streets and from the windows of adjacent buildings, Sadowski unhesitatingly returned to his tank and endeavored to pry up the bow gunner's hatch.

"The gallant and noble sacrifice"

"While engaged in this attempt to rescue his comrade from the burning tank, he was cut down by a stream of machine-gun fire which resulted in his death. The gallant and noble sacrifice of his life in the aid of his comrade, undertaken in the face of almost certain death, so inspired the remainder of the tank crews that they pressed forward with great ferocity and completely destroyed the enemy forces in this town without further loss to themselves. The heroism and selfless devotion to duty displayed by Sadowski, which resulted in his death, inspired the remainder of his force to press forward to victory,

and reflect the highest tradition of the armed forces."

For another three days, the 3rd and 15th Panzergrenadier Divisions tried to push the 4th Armored and 80th Infantry Divisions back across the Moselle, but Eddy's men were too strong for them and the two German units only managed to exhaust themselves in the process, losing hundreds of casualties in fruitless attacks. With Nancy in danger of being cut off, Blaskowitz ordered the city evacuated, and in a couple of days it was abandoned. It fell to the 35th Infantry Division's Task Force "S" to liberate the city, as recalled in the regimental history of the 134th Infantry.

"At 11:10 hours the first American tanks, carrying men of the 134th Infantry, arrived. Within 20 minutes a new *commissaire de la republique*, M. Chailley-Bert, was installed, and immediately he issued a proclamation to the population: 'NANCY IS FREE, but the battle is continuing at the gates of the city where Frenchmen and Americans are uniting their efforts'. When a wandering German officer had gone into Nancy during the last days of the occupation, according to a story in the *New York Sun*, he had found the city full of German troops, unconscious of their doom, drinking and singing, playing musical instruments, and dancing with and making love to French girls. Not till the

bullets began to whiz about their ears in Nancy did the Germans suspect that these French girls who were ostensibly fraternizing with them, were secret agents of the Resistance, waiting to hear news of orders for them to pull out. That was the signal for street fighting to begin. You had to be on the inside of the underground to know that. Now, as the 134th Infantry moved into the city, wild, happy throngs lined the streets, and crowds filled the great open square – Place Stanislas – to acclaim the liberators. There were still some snipers and small groups for the 1st Battalion to clean out, while excited Frenchmen ran about seeking to ferret out snipers, German stragglers, collaborators."

■ *Above:* US infantry of the Third Army, supported by armoured elements, put in an assault near the village of Dombasle.

During the second week of September 1944, the reinforcements promised to Patton by Bradley at last began to near the Lorraine battlefield. Wade Haislip's XV Corps had been fighting north of Paris with Courtney Hodges' First Army in late August, and was now heading for the southern flank of the Third Army, to achieve a link-up with the US Seventh Army, which was advancing from the south of France.

Haislip was perhaps Patton's most aggressive corps commander, and he had his sights set on destroying the German LXIV Corps, which was occupying a salient pointing westwards, south of Nancy. After linking up with the Seventh Army on 10 September and completing a continuous Allied front from the English Channel to the Mediterranean Sea, Haislip moved eastwards to strike at the Germans.

His first target was the German 16th Infantry Division, guarding the approaches to Dompaire. The US 79th Infantry Division struck at the German front, while the veteran Free French 2nd Armoured Division infiltrated through

a weakly held sector of the line to encircle the 16th Division. Acting on intelligence from local people, the Free French tank units quickly found a route past the German defences, and by late on 12 September they were approaching Dompaire, deep behind the 16th Division's front.

Blaskowitz now committed his armoured reserves in the sector, the 112th Panzer Brigade, with more than 38 Panthers, and 45 Panzer IV tanks of the 21st Panzer Division, backed up by a regiment of infantry.

Like its counterpart, the 106th Brigade, the 112th Brigade was a green outfit that was poorly trained and not really ready for combat. The Germans used the cover of darkness to move their tanks into Dompaire but the noise of the column alerted the nearby French troops, who moved their own tanks into hull-down fire positions.

At daybreak, an American forward air controller with the Free French troops started to direct a steady stream of P-47 Thunderbolts into action against the German tanks in villages

■ *Above:* A knocked-out German tank. As the Third Army moved eastwards, Patton made sure that Weyland's planes had forward bases from which to continue smashing German armour in the field.

around Dompaire. Rockets, bombs and machine-gun fire rained down on the Germans, destroying eight Panthers and prompting several inexperienced crews to abandon their vehicles to seek cover. Under cover of more air strikes the French moved forward to block all the escape routes of 112th Brigade.

The P-47, a quite remarkable aircraft, was again showing its worth to the Third Army. P-47s often came back from combat shot full of holes, their wings and control surfaces in tatters. On one occasion a Thunderbolt pilot, Lieutenant Chetwood, hit a steel pole after strafing a train over occupied France. The collision sliced 1.21m (4ft) off one of his wings, yet he was able to fly back safely to his base in England. A typical armament load was six or eight

.5in wing-mounted Browning machine guns with 267 or 425 rounds per gun and up to 1136kg (2500lb) of bombs or 10 5in rockets.

The 21st Panzer Division now intervened, attacking from the south and threatening to outflank the Free French advance guard. Determined resistance from a handful of Shermans, M10 tank destroyers and machine gun-equipped jeeps held the German tanks at bay for several key hours and broke up a panzergrenadier attack.

On the afternoon of 13 September, the trapped 112th Brigade tried to counterattack out of Dompaire, only to be beaten back with heavy losses to hull-down Shermans and more P-47 attacks. By the evening the German attack force was in full retreat, after losing almost

■ *Below:* **A heavily camouflaged US M10 tank destroyer lies in ambush somewhere in the Lorraine area.**

two-thirds of its tank force. The 112th brigade had lost 34 of its Panthers and the 21st Panzer was reduced to only 17 operational tanks. This débâcle doomed the German LXIV Corps, whose survivors were soon heading for safety at top speed. Within days Haislip's men were on the Moselle.

The loss of Nancy and defeat of LXIV Corps put on hold Hitler's plans for an all-out offensive against Patton, and Blaskowitz managed to persuade the Führer to use the remaining panzer reserves in local counterattacks to restore the situation.

General of Panzer Troops Hasso von Manteuffel was given the job of blunting Patton's attack. His Fifth Panzer Army was to be reinforced with the 11th Panzer Division and the 111th and 113th Panzer Brigades to allow it to defeat and drive back the 4th Armored Division, which had pushed eastward from Nancy to Arracourt and Lunéville. The 11th Panzer was still en route and would not take part in the initial assault.

The German offensive began on 18 September. In a series of skirmishes with American scout units the two panzer brigades failed to make significant gains. During the night, Manteuffel called off his thrust to Lunéville and concentrated his forces against the 4th Armored's Combat Command A. The German

■ *Above:* **The crew of a US Hellcat keeps a watchful eye for German troops in the town of Lunéville.**

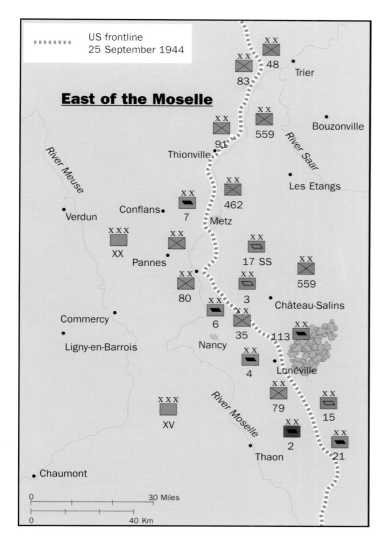

US frontline
25 September 1944

East of the Moselle

Trier

48

83

559

Bouzonville

91

Thionville

559

Les Etangs

462

Conflans

7

Metz

Verdun

XX

Pannes

17 SS

559

80

3

Château-Salins

Commercy

6

35

113

Ligny-en-Barrois

Nancy

4

Lunéville

79

15

XV

2

Thaon

21

Chaumont

0   30 Miles
0   40 Km

■ *Above:* The disposition of Patton's forces at the end of September 1944. Having forced its way across the River Moselle, the Third Army still faced sizeable German resistance.

attack went in under thick morning fog, which effectively blinded both sides.

The 113th Panzer Brigade spearheaded the German attack, and in the fog it had several inconclusive engagements with isolated groups of Colonel Clarke's tanks defending Arracourt. Panthers and Shermans blundered around in the fog, opening fire at ranges under 100m (328ft). Eleven Panthers were lost in these battles as the American tank crews exploited their superior local knowledge and radio communications to spring repeated ambushes on their opponents.

Later in the morning the German column then ran into M18 Hellcats of

the 704th Tank Destroyer Battalion, which claimed another 19 German tanks knocked out. The M18 was one of the fastest armored fighting vehicles of World War II, having a maximum road speed of 80km/h (50mph). This was mainly due to a combination of light weight, a sturdy Christie-based suspension and a 400hp engine, all combining to provide a high power-to-weight ratio. Its light weight was partly due to its light armour, as it was intended that the M18 would utilize its speed and mobility for "shoot and scoot" tactics. The light armour was partially offset by the arrangement of the sloping armour plates to provide extra protection. It was one of the best all-round tank destroyers of World War II.

Colonel Abrams then mustered a counterattack force of Shermans to strike at the remaining German tanks. When Patton visited the battlefield in the afternoon, John Wood reported that his troopers had knocked out 43 Panthers for the loss of three M18s and five Shermans.

A steady advance

Clarke's tanks had been able to concentrate their efforts against the 113th Brigade because the 111th Panzer Brigade, which was supposed to strike against the 4th Armored in a concerted attack, got lost in the fog and was unable to get into action.

During the following day, Wood ordered his tanks to counterattack against the remnants of the 113th Brigade. By now, the other German panzer column had found its way and struck out of the fog against rear-echelon elements of the 4th Armor. A field artillery battalion eventually halted the German attack when it deployed its 155mm howitzers in the direct-fire role.

Abrams's 37th Tank Battalion was swung south to counterattack against this new threat. The unit's first foray was

driven off for the loss of six Shermans when it was ambushed by German Panzer IV medium tanks. After regrouping, Abrams' troopers attacked again and this time they got the better of the Germans, knocking out 11 Panthers for 6 more Shermans. Five more German tanks were knocked out as the attack rolled on.

The battlefield was largely quiet on 21 September as the Germans reorganized their forces for a new attack, against the northern flank of Combat Command A the following day. Thick fog shielded the 111th Panzer Brigade from Allied airpower, and so the burden of the defence fell on M18 tank destroyers. When the fog finally lifted

later in the day, swarms of P-47s were able to interdict for the first time in several days. Their intervention delayed the German column long enough for the 37th Tank Battalion to get into position on the prominent ridge to begin engaging the advancing Panthers. The Germans were caught in a killing zone: pounded with artillery, hit by air strikes and then engaged by Shermans. By the end of the day the 111th Brigade was reduced to 7 tanks and 90 men from its strength of 90 tanks and 2500 men three days before. The 4th Armored had successfully fought off a numerically superior force for the loss of only 14 Shermans and 7 M5 light tanks, 25 killed and 88 wounded.

■ *Above:* **Though Patton's Third Army was famous for its armoured units, it relied heavily on the skills of its supporting artillery to blunt panzer counterattacks.**

On the 4th Armored's northern flank, the 35th Infantry Division was heavily engaged expanding the bridge-head across the Moselle against determined German resistance in a series of villages and wooded hillsides.

The 6th Armored attacks

The first elements of the 6th Armored Division were now committed to the battle after their long march from Brittany. The 134th Regiment's official history describes the engagement:

"Combat Command B of the 6th Armored Division was attached to the 35th, and on the morning of 22 September it was located north and in the rear of the enemy in the Chapenoux woods. At noon a coordinated attack began. Following a heavy artillery preparation and air strike, the tanks of the 35th Division's 737th Tank Battalion moved in with the infantry riding on them. The Germans met the attack from dug-in positions on the southern edge of the woods in an unbroken string of emplacements, each having an almost perfect field of fire. With a network of trails leading in and out of the woods, accessibility of supplies was facilitated and it was possible for the enemy to move tanks out to the fringe of the woods to fire, and then withdraw to another position. Once, however, the strongpoints on the edges of the woods were cracked, the main resistance would be broken. Jumping off the tanks as they approached the woods, the 137th drove into the position and prepared for hand-to-hand combat. In less than an hour they had forced the enemy to withdraw and began the pursuit through the woods. Then Combat Command B of the 6th Armored began closing the trap from the rear. American tanks were barking in all directions as the German withdrawal became a rout. The roads from Moulins to Bouxieres-aux-Chênes

became a choked mass of enemy motor and horse-drawn artillery as the 134th charged forward from the hills east of the town of Nancy.

"Hastening enemy troops struggled through the already packed highways, in some instances with columns [six and a half kilometers] four miles long. The 134th reported this mass retreat and air forces went to work on the fleeing Germans, strafing and bombing at will. Elements of the 137th not only took the woods, but also swung left and captured Amance and the high ground in order to forestall any further German concentration in that sector. Throughout the next two days the Division continued to mop up the area, taking many prisoners and great quantities of booty."

The supply problem

As Colonel Clarke's men were fighting off the panzer attack, Patton was informed by Bradley that there were no longer enough supplies to continue the Third Army's offensive. The British had launched an airborne offensive into Holland – Operation Market Garden – and they would now receive the bulk of the Allied fuel and ammunition for the coming weeks. XV Corps and the 6th Armored were also being pulled away from the Third Army at the end of the month. On 23 September, Patton met his corps commanders to plan how to reorientate his forces for a general defensive battle.

Even before they had time to put their plans into action, Manteuffel struck again, sending the newly arrived 11th Panzer Division into action against 4th Armored, while the 559th Volks-grenadier Division and the reinforced 106th Panzer Brigade hit the 35th Infantry Division. Two regiments of German infantry, backed up by tanks, were threatening to overwhelm the 4th Armored's Combat Command B when two squadrons of P-47s dived below low cloud cover in a daredevil attack that won one of the pilots a Medal of Honor recommendation from Patton himself. In the space of 15 minutes the Thunderbolts killed 300 Germans and knocked out 11 tanks.

The next day, the 11th Panzer threw 50 tanks into action and forced the 4th Armored to pull back to a more defensible line. After a day's rest Manteuffel struck again with a force of 24 Panthers and 6 Panzer IVs, backed up by several infantry regiments, from the south against Hills 318 and 265. For three days the battle see-sawed with attacks and counterattacks raging around the Lorraine countryside.

Blunting the panzers

Both sides suffered hundreds of casualties in the vicious fighting, but in the end superior American artillery and airpower won the day and Manteuffel eventually called off his attacks. The Germans lost 700 killed and 300 wounded in four days of fighting against the 4th Armored, along with 22 Panthers and 14 Panzer IVs destroyed. In the fighting around Arracourt the Germans lost 86 tanks and more than 100 were badly damaged. Wood's division lost 41 Shermans and 7 M5A1 light tanks, as well as suffering 225 killed and 648 wounded.

Blaskowitz had paid with his job for his failure to retake Nancy, and on 29 September his successor, General of Panzer Troops Hermann Balck, ordered Manteuffel to pull the 11th Panzer out of the line to refit. Patton's troops had held their ground.

The fighting did not die down, though. Two more German divisions, the 15th Panzergrenadier and 599th Volksgrenadier, hit the 35th Infantry on 30 September and forced it back. Patton ordered the newly arrived 6th Armored to counterattack and restore the situation. Eddy and the 6th Armored's

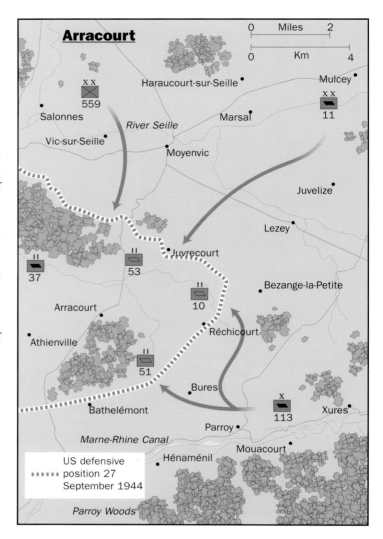

commander, Robert Grow, were almost killed by German shell fire. When Patton arrived to inspect the situation he was enraged that the badly shaken Eddy had ordered two regiments to retreat, calling him a "disgrace". He demanded that Grow personally lead his troops in the counterattack to regain the lost ground, "or not come back". The attack restored the situation.

As the fighting around Nancy was reaching its climax, XX Corps again tried to blast its way through to Metz. On 27 September, Patton's heavy artillery and aircraft dropping 1000lb bombs and napalm saturated the defences of Fort Driant, which guarded

■ *Above:* **The battle that raged around the town of Arracourt in September 1944. Though Manteuffel drove back the US forces, he was unable to retake Nancy itself.**

the southern approaches to Metz, before the 11th Infantry Regiment was launched forward again backed by Sherman tanks. After a fierce day of fighting little progress was made and the GIs pulled back to their start line under the cover of darkness.

In a bloody month of fighting the Third Army had crossed the River Moselle and inflicted heavy losses on the German forces sent to halt its advance. The Germans lost some 220 tanks and 220 assault guns in the fighting, which they could ill afford, while Patton had lost 49 light tanks and 151 Shermans, losses that could be replaced with relative ease. This had been the Third

Army's toughest battle since it broke out of Normandy at the end of July.

Patton's ambition to break through to the River Rhine had proved illusory because of the lack of supplies. The month-long battle proved that Patton's men were more than capable of taking on the Germans in a stand-up fight, and refuted criticism that they were only good for chasing defeated units. The Battle for Lorraine was far from over, however. Patton's men would spend another two miserable months locked in frustrating battles to try to batter through the Siegfield Line and into Germany. And all the while the weather was deteriorating as winter approached.

CONCLUSION

THE RECORD

"Third Army had advanced farther and faster than any army in history."

General Patton, 14 August 1944

Command of the US Third Army during the French campaign was the pinnacle of George Patton's military career. He was in his element, leading his troops in their "hell-for-leather" breakout from Normandy. Patton undoubtedly enjoyed himself immensely, and even titled the chapter in his memories on the campaign, "Touring France with an Army".

In the two months after his Third Army was unleashed, Patton put his theories of armoured warfare into practice. He outflanked, outfought and out-thought his opponents from Avranches to the River Moselle. Not without justification is Patton's advance dubbed an "American Blitzkrieg". The rapid advance of the Third Army kept the German forces in France off-balance from the moment Patton's troops entered the battle. A succession of Hitler's top generals were unable to successfully counter Patton's tactics, and it was only when the Third Army approached France's eastern border – and outran its supply lines – that the German Army was able to get its act together and stabilize the front.

Patton was keen to quantify his troop's achievements and had his staff keep copious records of the Third Army's combat statistics. Up to 1 October 1944 it had lost 4849 men killed in action, had 24,585 wounded and recorded 5092 as missing. It had also lost 14,637 non-battle casualties. In combat it had lost 143 light tanks and 363 medium tanks, as well as 103 artillery pieces. For these modest losses, Patton claimed his

■ *Left:* **General Patton accepts the plaudits from a grateful Parisian population. He is seen here after having attended a ceremony handing back recaptured French flags.**

troops killed 32,900 Germans and wounded a further 99,300. A total of 96,500 German troops were captured by the Third Army. Some 808 German medium tanks and 439 Panther and Tiger heavy tanks were claimed destroyed by the Third Army, along with 1751 artillery pieces.

XIX Tactical Air Command contributed immensely to the devastation wrought by the Third Army, including 163 confirmed kills in air-to-air combat and a further 66 German aircraft destroyed on the ground. Otto Weyland's fighter-bombers claimed 4058 motor vehicles, 466 tanks and other armour, 598 horse-drawn vehicles, 256 locomotives and 2,956 wagons destroyed on the ground in 12,292 sorties, along with 155 barges and other naval craft, 18 merchant vessels and 8 naval vessels. This tally was achieved for the loss of 114 US aircraft.

The key to success

Patton's success was due to a combination of his aggressive adoption of Blitzkrieg-style tactics, integration of airpower, armour and intelligence from Ultra, and his motivational skills.

The Third Army put into practice a number of highly innovative tactics and procedures for armour–air cooperation with considerable flair. Patton, along with key subordinates like Manton Eddy, Wade Haislip, Otto Weyland, John Wood and Robert Grow, showed they were experts in the art of mechanized offensive warfare.

At the heart of the Third Army was Patton's extraordinary ability to "read" a battle. He could judge how a battle was flowing and had at his disposal a finely tuned instrument – the Third Army – that could rapidly react to the constant stream of new ideas that originated from its commander.

Patton grew in confidence as the campaign in France progressed, and he

■ *Left:* General Patton with his faithful dog Willie. Not long after tasting triumph in the Allied victory over Germany, Patton was to lose his life following a tragic road traffic accident.

became expert at taking calculated risks to ensure his armoured spearheads were kept free to keep the Germans continually off-balance.

The Third Army's divisions had an unusually high level of *esprit de corps* which kept it fighting continuously through August and September, when many other US Army formations were worn out by continuous combat. Patton was unmistakably the leader of the Third Army, and his men showed they were willing to follow him through thick and thin.

Controversy

Patton's contribution to the Allied victory in Normandy is clouded in controversy. In the aftermath of the victory at Falaise, argument has raged over whether Bradley was right to halt Patton on 13 August. Critics have pointed to the fact that all the major German headquarters and panzer divisions managed to escape with strong cadres of officers and specialist troops intact. These men later formed the basis of the rebuilt Wehrmacht that was able to strike at the Allies in the Ardennes in December 1944. If the pocket had been closed a week earlier these fanatical Nazis would not have escaped, claimed Bradley's critics.

Despite Patton's boasts that he could have easily closed the Falaise Gap with XV Corps, the heavy fighting to close the pocket indicates that the Germans were far from defeated.

However, Allied forces inflicted horrendous losses on the Germans trapped inside the pocket, and few of the troops that escaped were in any physical or mental shape to put up serious resistance for several months. Those criticizing Bradley perhaps have unrealistic expectations. For the German troops streaming eastwards from Falaise, they had no doubt that they had been soundly defeated.

In the final weeks of August and into September 1944, Patton was constantly arguing with Bradley and Eisenhower that their "broad front" strategy was flawed. He claimed that if his Third Army had received a higher priority for supplies he could have punched through to the Rhine and knocked Germany out of the war by the end of 1944.

This was exactly the argument made by Montgomery to support his failed Arnhem offensive in September 1944. The German Wehrmacht proved far more resilient than the Allies expected, and it was far from clear that Patton would have been any more successful than Monty. We shall never know.

The legacy

Though Patton's relentless thrusts were over by late September 1944, he and his army still had crucial roles to play in the war. When German forces launched their Ardennes counteroffensive in December 1944, the famous Battle of the Bulge, Patton was able to drive his army northwards to the southern flank of the bulge and contain the enemy. Following this action, the Third Army was able to punch into southern Germany before heading into Czechoslovakia, freeing the city of Pilsen just before Germany surrendered on 8 May 1945.

Patton's campaign in France firmly established him as one of the most successful combat commanders of the twentieth century. His death following a road traffic accident in December 1945 robbed the US Army of one of its greatest generals. Had he lived, and managed to cope with peacetime soldiering for the interwar years, he would have undoubtedly been a great asset to the US forces in Korea. The US Army took Patton to its heart as its premier exponent of armoured warfare, naming its tank training centre in Kentucky after him.

US INFANTRY DIVISION

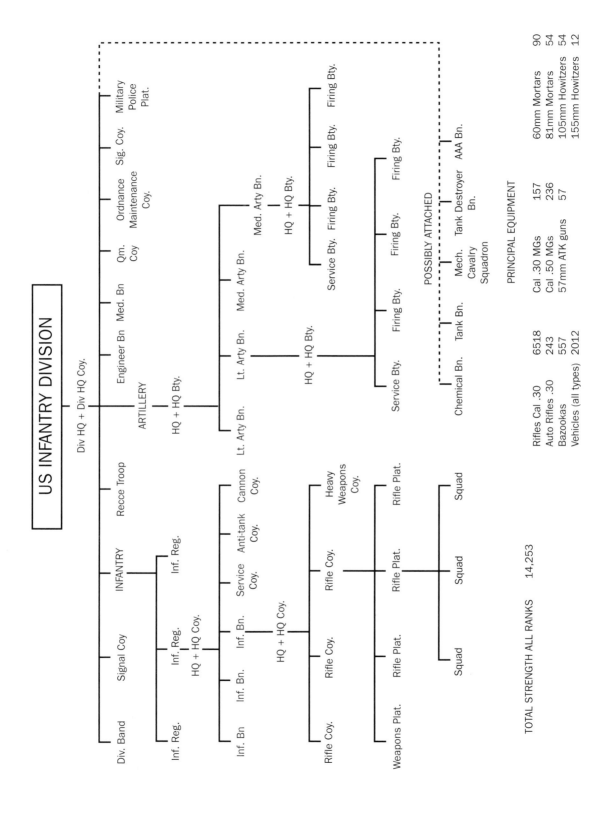

Div HQ + Div HQ Coy.

Div. Band — **Signal Coy** — **INFANTRY** — **Recce Troop** — **ARTILLERY** — **Engineer Bn** — **Med. Bn** — **Qm. Coy** — **Ordnance Maintenance Coy.** — **Sig. Coy.** — **Military Police Plat.**

INFANTRY:
Inf. Reg. — Inf. Reg. — Inf. Reg.

HQ + HQ Coy.
Inf. Reg.: Inf. Bn — Inf. Bn. — Inf. Bn. — Service Coy. — Anti-tank Coy. — Cannon Coy.

HQ + HQ Coy.
Inf. Bn: Rifle Coy. — Rifle Coy. — Rifle Coy. — Heavy Weapons Coy.

Rifle Coy.: Weapons Plat. — Rifle Plat. — Rifle Plat. — Rifle Plat.

Rifle Plat.: Squad — Squad — Squad

ARTILLERY:
HQ + HQ Bty.
Lt. Arty Bn. — Lt. Arty Bn. — Med. Arty Bn.

HQ + HQ Bty.
Service Bty. — Firing Bty. — Firing Bty. — Firing Bty.

Med. Arty Bn.:
HQ + HQ Bty.
Service Bty. — Firing Bty. — Firing Bty. — Firing Bty.

POSSIBLY ATTACHED

Chemical Bn. — Tank Bn. — Mech. Cavalry Squadron — Tank Destroyer Bn. — AAA Bn.

PRINCIPAL EQUIPMENT

Rifles Cal .30	6518	Cal .30 MGs	157	60mm Mortars	90
Auto Rifles .30	243	Cal .50 MGs	236	81mm Mortars	54
Bazookas	557	57mm ATK guns	57	105mm Howitzers	54
Vehicles (all types)	2012			155mm Howitzers	12

TOTAL STRENGTH ALL RANKS   14,253

US ARMORED DIVISION

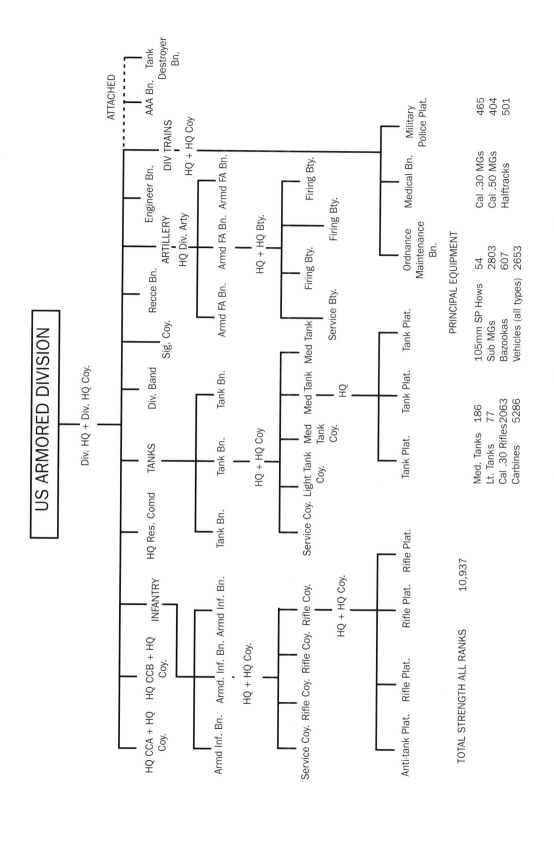

Div. HQ + Div. HQ Coy.

INFANTRY
- HQ CCA + HQ Coy.
- HQ CCB + HQ Coy.

HQ Res. Comd

Div. Band

Sig. Coy.

Recce Bn.

ARTILLERY
- HQ Div. Arty

Engineer Bn.

DIV TRAINS
- HQ + HQ Coy

ATTACHED
- AAA Bn.
- Tank Destroyer Bn.

Armd Inf. Bn. — Armd. Inf. Bn. — Armd Inf. Bn.
- HQ + HQ Coy.

Service Coy. — Rifle Coy. — Rifle Coy. — Rifle Coy.
- HQ + HQ Coy.

Anti-tank Plat. — Rifle Plat. — Rifle Plat. — Rifle Plat.

TANKS
- Tank Bn. — Tank Bn. — Tank Bn.
- HQ + HQ Coy

Service Coy. — Light Tank Coy. — Med Tank Coy. — Med Tank — Med Tank
- HQ

Tank Plat. — Tank Plat. — Tank Plat. — Tank Plat.

Armd FA Bn. — Armd FA Bn. — Armd FA Bn.
- HQ + HQ Bty.

Firing Bty. — Firing Bty. — Firing Bty. — Firing Bty.

Service Bty.

Ordnance Maintenance Bn. — Medical Bn. — Military Police Plat.

PRINCIPAL EQUIPMENT

Med. Tanks	186
Lt. Tanks	77
Cal .30 Rifles	2063
Carbines	5286
105mm SP Hows	54
Sub MGs	2803
Bazookas	607
Vehicles (all types)	2653
Cal .30 MGs	465
Cal .50 MGs	404
Halftracks	501

TOTAL STRENGTH ALL RANKS   10,937

4th ARMORED DIVISION

Major-General John Wood

COMPOSITION

Organic units

Headquarters Company
Reserve Command
Combat Command A
Combat Command B
8th Tank Battalion
35th Tank Battalion
37th Tank Battalion
10th Armored Infantry Battalion
51st Armored Infantry Battalion
53rd Armored Infantry Battalion
25th Cavalry Recon Squadron (Mechanized)
24th Armored Engineer Battalion
144th Armored Signal Company
4th Armored Division Artillery
22nd Armored Field Artillery Battalion
66th Armored Field Artillery Battalion
94th Armored Field Artillery Battalion
4th Armored Division Trains
126th Ordnance Maintenance Battalion
4th Armored Medical Battlion
Military Police Platoon
Band

Attachments

489th Anti-aircraft Artillery Battalion
Co A 86th Chemical Mortar Battalion
995th Engr Treadway Bridging Company
77th, 179th, 191st, 216th, 219, 253rd, 695th, 696th FA Battalions
5th, 177th Field Artillery Groups
13th, 137th, 319th, 230th Infantry Regiments
1st Battalion, 318th Infantry Regiment
2nd Battalion, 320th Infantry Regiment

5th ARMORED DIVISION
"Victory"

Major-General Lundsford E. Oliver

COMPOSITION

Organic units
Headquarters Company
Reserve Command
Combat Command A
Combat Command B
10th Tank Battalion
34th Tank Battalion
81st Tank Battalion
15th Armored Infantry Battalion
46th Armored Infantry Battalion
47th Armored Infantry Battalion
85th Cavalry Rcn Sq (Mechanized)
22nd Armored Engineer Battalion
145th Armored Signal Company
5th Armored Division Artillery
47th Armored Field Artillery Battalion
71st Armored Field Artillery Battalion
95th Armored Field Artillery Battalion
5th Armored Division Trains
127th Ordnance Maintenance Battalion
75th Armored Medical Battalion
Military Police Platoon
Band

Attachments
387th Anti-aircraft Artillery Battalion
208th, 975th, 987th Field Artillery Battalions
400th Armored Field Artillery Battalion
628th Tank Destroyer Battalion

6th ARMORED DIVISION
"Super Sixth"

Major-General Robert W. Grow

COMPOSITION
Organic units

Headquarters Company
Reserve Command
Combat Command A
Combat Command B
15th Tank Battalion
68th Tank Battalion
69th Tank Battalion
9th Armored Infantry Battalion
44th Armored Infantry Battalion
50th Armored Infantry Battalion
86th Cavalry Rcn Sq (Mechanized)
25th Armored Engineer Battalion
146th Armored Signal Company
6th Armored Division Artillery
128th Armored Field Artillery Battalion
212th Armored Field Artillery Battalion
231st Armored Field Artillery Battalion
6th Armored Division Trains
128th Ordnance Maintenance Battalion
76th Armored Medical Battalion
Military Police Platoon
Band

Attachments
777th Anti-aircraft Artillery Battalion
965th, 969th, 45th, 28th Field Artillery Battalions
83rd, 174th Armored Field Artillery Battalions
28th, 134th Infantry Battalions

5th INFANTRY DIVISION
"Red Diamond Division"

Major-General S. Leroy Irwin

COMPOSITION
Organic units
2d Infantry Regiment
10th Infantry Regiment
11th Infantry Regiment
5th Reconnaissance Troop (Mechanized)
7th Engineer Combat Battalion
5th Medical Battalion
5th Division Artillery
19th Field Artillery Battalion (105mm Howitzer)
46th Field Artillery Battalion (105mm Howitzer)
50th Field Artillery Battalion (105mm Howitzer)
21st Field Artillery Battalion (155mm Howitzer)
Special Troops
705th Ordnance Light Maintenance Company
5th Quartermaster Company
5th Signal Company
Military Police Platoon
Headquarters Company
Band

Attachments
449th Anti-aircraft Artillery Battalionn
Battery D 116th AAA Gun Battalion (Mobile)
735th Tank Battalion
3rd, 38th Cavalry Reconnaissance Squadrons
81st Chemical Mortar Battalion, 84th Chemical SG Company
150th Combat Engineer Battalion, 994th Engineer Treadway Bridging Company
537th, 509th Engineer Light Pontoon Companies, 160th Combat Engineer Battalion
989th Engineer Treadway Bridging Company
187th, 204th, 282nd, 241st, 284th, 434th Field Artillery Battalions
7th FA Observation Battalion
5th Ranger Infantry Battalion
3rd Battalion, 8th Infantry Regiment
818th, 774th Tank Destroyer Battalions

8th INFANTRY DIVISION
"Pathfinder Division"
"Arrow Division"

Major-General Donald A. Stroh

COMPOSITION
Organic units
13th Infantry Regiment
28th Infantry Regiment
121st Infantry Regiment
8th Reconnaissance Troop (Mechanized)
12th Engineer Combat Battalion
8th Medical Battalion
8th Division Artillery
43rd Field Artillery Battalion (105mm Howitzer)
45th Field Artillery Battalion (105mm Howitzer)
56th Field Artillery Battalion (105mm Howitzer)
28th Field Artillery Battalion (155mm Howitzer)
Special Troops
708th Ordnance Light Maintenance Company
8th Quartermaster Company
8th Signal Company
Military Police Platoon
Headquarters Company
Band

Attachments
445th Anti-aircraft Artillery Battalion (Mobile)
709th Tank Battalion
86th Chemical Mortar Battalion
174th, 196th, 402nd Field Artillery Groups
2nd Ranger Infantry Battalion
644th Tank Destroyer Battalion

35th INFANTRY DIVISION
"Sante Fe Division"

Major-General Paul W. Baade

COMPOSITION
Organic units
134th Infantry Regiment
137th Infantry Regiment
320th Infantry Regiment
35th Reconnaissance Troop (Mechanized)
60th Engineer Combat Battalion
110th Medical Battalion
35th Division Artillery
161st Field Artillery Battalion (105mm Howitzer)
216th Field Artillery Battalion (105mm Howitzer)
219th Field Artillery Battalion (105mm Howitzer)
127th Field Artillery Battalion (155mm Howitzer)
Special Troops
735th Ordnance Light Maintenance Company
35th Quartermaster Company
35th Signal Company
Military Police Platoon
Headquarters Company
Band

Attachments
448th, 459th, 116th Anti-aircraft Battalions (Mobile)
69th, 737th Tank Battalions
Company D, 32nd Armored Regiment
44th, 212th Armored Infantry Battalions
Troop B, 86th Cavalry Reconnaissance Squadron
Company C, 25th Armored Engineer Battalion
4th Cavalry Reconnaissance Squadron
106th Cavalry Group
81st, 82nd, 86th Chemical Mortar Battalions
183rd, 255th, 967th, 974th Field Artillery Battalions
29th Division Artillery
182nd Field Artillery Group
654th, 821st, 691st Tank Destroyer Battalions

79th INFANTRY DIVISION
"Cross of Lorraine Division"

Major-General Ira T. Wyche

COMPOSITION
313th Infantry Regiment
314th Infantry Regiment
315th Infantry Regiment
79th Reconnaissance Troop (Mechanized)
304th Engineer Combat Battalion
304th Medical Battalion
79th Division Artillery
310th Field Artillery Battalion (105mm Howitzer)
311th Field Artillery Battalion (105mm Howitzer)
904th Field Artillery Battalion (105mm Howitzer)
312th Field Artillery Battalion (155mm Howitzer)
Special Troops
779th Ordnance Light Maintenance Company
79th Quartermaster Company
79th Signal Company
Military Police Platoon
Headquarters Company
Band

Attachments
749th Tank Battalion
813th Tank Destroyer Battalion
773rd Tank Destroyer Battalion

80th INFANTRY DIVISION
"Blue Ridge Division"

Major-General Horace L. McBride

COMPOSITION
317th Infantry Regiment
318th Infantry Regiment
319th Infantry Regiment
80th Reconnaissance Troop (Mechanized)
305th Engineer Combat Battalion
305th Medical Battalion
80th Division Artillery
313th Field Artillery Battalion (105mm Howitzer)
314th Field Artillery Battalion (105mm Howitzer)
905th Field Artillery Battalion (105mm Howitzer)
315th Field Artillery Battalion (155mm Howitzer)
Special Troops
780th Ordnance Light Maintenance Company
80th Quartermaster Company
80th Signal Company
Military Police Platoon
Headquarters Company
Band

Attachments
633rd Anti-aircraft Artillery Battalion (Mobile)
702nd Tank Battalion
610th, 691st, 808th Tank Destroyer Battalions

90th INFANTRY DIVISION
"Alamo Division"
"Tough Ombres"

Major-General Raymond S. McLain

Organic units
357th Infantry Regiment
358th Infantry Regiment
359th Infantry Regiment
90th Reconnaissance Troop (Mechanized)
325th Engineer Combat Battalion
315th Medical Battalion
90th Division Artillery
343rd Field Artillery Battalion (105mm Howitzer)
344th Field Artillery Battalion (105mm Howitzer)
915th Field Artillery Battalion (105mm Howitzer)
345th Field Artillery Battalion (105mm Howitzer)
Special Troops
790th Ordnance Light Maintenance Company
90th Quartermaster Company
90th Signal Company
Military Police platoon
Headquarters Company
Band

Attachments
537th Anti-aircraft Artillery AW Battalion (Mobile)
17th, 712th Tank Battalions
1 CC French 2nd Armored Division
3rd, 4th, 43rd Cavalry Reconnaissance Squadrons
Cos C & D 81st Chemical Mortar Battalion
202nd, 282nd, 284th, 693rd, 999th Field Artillery Battalions
40th, 173rd Field Artillery Group
400th Armored Field Artillery Battalion
3rd Field Artillery Observation Battalion
607th, 803rd Tank Destroyer Battalions

US THIRD ARMY ORDER OF BATTLE AUGUST–SEPTEMBER 1944

DRIVE TO LE MANS (1–14 AUGUST 1944)
6th Cavalry Group (Colonel M Fitchett)
VIII Corps (Middleton, from First Army)
Task Force A
4th Armored Division
6th Armored Division
83rd Infantry Division (from 3rd)
79th Infantry Division
8th Infantry Division

XV Corps (Haislip)
5th Armored Division
79th Infantry Division
83rd Infantry Division (up to 3 Augst)
90th Infantry Division
2nd French Armored Division (attached 8 Aug)

XX Corps (Laval) (Walker)
7th Armored Division
5th Infantry Division
35th Infantry Division
80th Infantry Division (from 7 August)

XII Corps (Cook)
80th Infantry Division (up to 7 August)

FALAISE GAP, DRIVE TO SEINE, CLEARING THE WEST BANK (14–26 AUGUST)
VIII Corps (Brittany)
Task Force A
6th Armored Division
83rd Infantry Division
8th Infantry Division

XV Corps (Haislip)
5th Armored Division
79th Infantry Division
2nd French Armored Division (to First Army for liberation of Paris)
90th Infantry Division

XX Corps (Walker)
7th Armored Division
5th Infantry Division

80th Infantry Division

XII Corps (Cook replaced by Eddy)
4th Armored Division
35th Infantry Division

TO THE REICH'S BORDER (26 AUGUST–5 SEPTEMBER)
VIII Corps (Brittany)
2nd Infantry Division
29th Infantry Division
8th Infantry Division
83rd Infantry Division

XV Corps (Haislip) (to First Army 24 August)
79th Infantry Division
90th Infantry Division

XX Corps (Walker)
7th Armored Division
5th Infantry Division
80th Infantry Division

XII Corps (Eddy)
4th Armored Division
35th Infantry Division

FIGHTING IN LORRAINE (5–30 SEPTEMBER)
XX Corps
2nd Cavalry Reconnaissance Group
7th Armored Division
5th Infantry Division
90th Infantry Division
83rd Infantry Division (mid-September)

XII Corps
106th Cavalry Reconnaissance Group
4th Armored Division
6th Armored Division
35th Infantry Division
80th Infantry Division

XV Corps
79th Infantry Division
2nd French Armored Division

BIBLIOGRAPHY

Bishop, Chris, *WWII: The Directory of Weapons*, Aerospace Publishing, London, 2000

Blumenson, Martin, *Breakout and Pursuit, Part V of the United States Army in World War II: European Theater of Operations,* US Government Printing Office, USA, 1961

Blumenson, Martin, *The Duel for France, 1944,* Da Capo Press, USA, 1963

Blumenson, Martin, *The Patton Papers, 1940-1945,* Da Capo Press, USA, 1974

Badsey, Stephen, *Normandy 1944,* Opsrey, London, 1990

Bradley, Omar N., *A Soldier's Story,* Rinehart Winston, New York: Holt, 1951

Burns, Lt. Robert J., and Dahl, Lt. John S., *Unit History of the 68th Tank Battalion*

Carrell, Paul, *Invasion – They're Coming!,* George Harrap, London, 1964

Civarra, M/Sgt. Nick O., *Seek, Strike, Destroy, the WW II unit history of 1st Platoon, Recon Co., 603rd Tank Destroyer Battalion, 6th Armored Division,* Germany, 1945

Cole, Hugh M., *The Lorraine Campaign. Part VI of the United States Army in World War II: European Theater of Operations,* Washington: GPO, 1950

DeBevoise, Charles P., *History of the 81st Tank Battalion,* 81st Tank Battalion Association, 1947

D'Este, Carlo, *Patton: A Genius For War*, Harpercollins, London 1996

Essame, H., *Patton: The Commander,* Purnell Books, London, 1974

Forty, George, *Patton's Third Army at War,* Ian Allan, London, 1978

Forty, George, *The Armies of George S. Patton,* Arms and Armour, London, 1996

Frankel, Nat, and Smith, Larry, *Patton's Best,* Hawthorn Books, New York, 1978

Griesback, Lt. Marc F., *Combat History of the 8th Infantry Division*, Army & Navy Publishers, Louisiana, 1945

Guderian, Heinz, *Panzer Leader*, Futura, London, 1979

Hamilton, Nigel, *Monty: Master of the Battlefield 1942–44*, Hamish Hamilton, London, 1983

Harris, Kevin, *The Thunderbolt Division, The Story of the Eighty Third*, Battery Press, Nashville, 2000

Hastings, Max, *Overlord*, Michael Joseph, London, 1984

Hastings, Max, *Das Reich*, Michael Joseph, London, 1981

Hillery, Vic, and Hurley, Emmerson, *Paths of Armor, The 5th Armored Division in World War Two*, Battery Press, Nashville

Hogg, Ian V., *Patton*, Bison Books, London, 1984

Hofmann, Dr. George F., *Super Sixth – The History of the 6th Armored Division in WW II*, Battery Press, Nashville, 1993

Hughes, Thomas Alexander, *Overlord*, Free Press, London, 1995

Keegan, John, *Six Armies in Normandy*, Pimlico, London, 1982

Lehmann, Rudolf, and Tiemann, Ralf, *The Liebstandarte IV/1*, JJ Fedorowicz, Manitoba, 1993

Lefèvre, Eric, *Panzers in Normandy: Then and Now*, After the Battle, London, 1984

Maranda, Corporal Albert O., *World War II Diary Major General Butler B. Miltonberger and Major James A. Huston, 134th Infantry Regiment – "All Hell Can't Stop Us"*, Transcribed by Roberta V. Russo, Palatine, Illinois

McKee, Alexander *Caen: Anvil of Victory*, Souvenir Press, London, 1964

Mellenthin, F.W., *Panzer Battles*, Futura, London, 1977

Meyer, Hubert, *Hitlerjugend*, JJ Fedorowicz, Manitoba, 1994

Lord Montgomery of El Alamein, *Normandy to the Baltic*, Hutchinson, London, 1947

Mudd, Captain J.L., *Development of the Tank-Infantry Team during World War II in Africa and Europe*, in *ARMOR Magazine*, Fort Levenworth, September–October 1999

Oliver, Major-General Lunsford E., *5th Armored Division After Action Report for August 1944*, US Army, 1944

Patton, General George S., *War As I Knew It*, Houghton Mifflin, Boston, 1975

Reynolds, Michael, *Steel Inferno*, Spellmount, Staplehurst, 1997

Reynolds, Michael, *Men of Steel*, Spellmount, Staplehurst, 1999

Ripley, Tim, *Steel Rain*, Spellmount, Staplehurst, 2001

Rohmer, Richard, *Patton's Gap*, Arms and Armour, London, 1981

Shwedo, Major Bradford J., *XIX Tactical Air Command and ULTRA*, School of Advanced Airpower Studies, Maxwell AFB, 2000

Vandergriff, Major Donald E., *How MG Wood's 4th Armored Division Stormed Across France Without Written Orders*, in *ARMOR Magazine*, Fort Levenworth, September–October 2000

Zaloga, Steven J., *Sherman*, Osprey, London, 1978

Zaloga, Steven J., *Operation Cobra 1944*, Osprey, Oxford, 2001

Zaloga, Steven J., *Lorraine 1944: Patton vs Manteuffel*, Osprey, Oxford, 2002

Zetterling, Niklas, *Normandy 1944*, JJ Fedorowicz, Manitoba, 2000

Wings at War No 5: Air Ground Team Work on the Western Front, Center for Air Force History, Washington DC, 1992

Records of the Wehrmacht Inspector of Panzer Troops German Reports Series, 18 Volumes, US Army History of the Second World War, Purnell & Sons, 1966–1974

INDEX